WALKING WITH JESUS

Spiritual meditations for pilgrims in a weary land on their way to glory!

by Mary Winslow

1774-1854

PART 1:

How often one word, a simple sentence, when applied by the Holy Spirit, gives comfort, and lifts one up! How much we need these helps all through our weary pilgrimage! We are such forgetful creatures; too often forgetting what we are, and what a God He is.

How poor and unsatisfying are all things here below; even the best and the loveliest! Oh, to walk more intimately with Him, to live above the world, and hold the creature with a looser hand, taking God's Word as our guiding light; our unfailing spring of comfort. God has eternally provided such a magnificent and holy heaven for us above, that He is jealous lest we should set our hearts too fondly and closely upon the attractions of earth. Therefore it is that He withers our gourds and breaks our cisterns; only to dislodge us here, and lead us to seek those things which are above, where Christ our treasure is.

Let us keep our eye and our hearts upon our blessed home. Earth is but a stage erected as our passage to the place Jesus has gone to prepare for us. What a place must that be which infinite power and love has engaged to provide! Oh, let us not lose sight of heaven for a moment. How prone are we to allow our minds and hearts (treacherous hearts!) to become entangled with the baubles of a dying world. No wonder Christ exhorted us to watch and pray. Heaven is our home; our happy home. We are but strangers and pilgrims here. Try and realize it. Let us keep ourselves ready to enter with Him to the marriage supper of the Lamb. In a little while, and we shall see Him, not as the 'Man of sorrows,' but the 'King in His beauty.' Then let us fight against earth and all its false attractions, for it passes away.

God is my Shepherd, and all my concerns are in His hands. Blessed, forever blessed, be His dear and holy name, who has looked with everlasting mercy on such a poor, vile sinner as me; and encouraged me with such sweet manifestations of His love, to trust my soul and all my interests in His hands!

The world and its 'nothings' are often a sad snare to God's saints. Oh that by faith we may overcome it all, and keep close to Jesus! We are not of the world. Let us try and not attend to its gewgaws! Keep a more steadfast, unwavering eye upon Christ. He has gone a little before us, and stands beckoning us to follow. Live for eternity! Let go your hold upon the world! Receive this exhortation from an aged pilgrim, who, as she nears the solemn scenes of eternity, and more realizes the inexpressible joys that await us there, is anxious that all the believers who are traveling the same road might have their hearts and minds more disentangled from earth and earthly things, and themselves unreservedly given to Christ. Let us aim in all things to follow Him who, despising this world's show, left us an example how we should walk. Have your lamp trimmed and brightly burning, for every day and every hour brings us nearer and nearer to our home!

"Dearest Jesus! help Your pilgrims to live more like pilgrims, above a poor dying world, and more in full view of the glory that awaits them when they shall see You face to face!"

The Christian Journey. Life is a journey, often a short one, and always uncertain. But there is another journey. The believer is traveling through a waste howling wilderness, to another and a glorious region, where ineffable delight and happiness await us. The road is narrow, the entrance strait, so strait that thousands miss it and perish in the wilderness. But true believers, under the teaching and convoy of the Holy Spirit, find it and walk in it. The King, in His infinite love and compassion, has made a hedge about them, separating and defending them from the many beasts of prey that lurk around them; and although they hear their howlings and behold their threatenings, they are safe from their power. But their strongest foe is within themselves; a heart deceitful above all things and desperately wicked. From this there is no escape but by constant watchfulness, and earnest cries to their best Friend and Guide for protection. Were it not for this faithful Guide, how often, discouraged by reason of the way, would they turn back! But He watches over them by night and by day, strengthens them when weak, upholds them when falling, encourages them when cast down, defends them when attacked, provides for them when in need, leads them by living streams, and causes them there to lie down in pleasant pastures, and on sunny banks. And as they advance they obtain brighter views of the good land they are nearing, and they long to see the King in His beauty, and the land that is yet very far off, and to meet those that have already arrived on that happy shore.

It is high time we awoke out of sleep, and aim to live more for eternity, to live more for God, and to God. With this world and its opinions and maxims, we, as believers, have nothing to do, for they are contrary to God's Word. And as it respects mere professing Christians, we had better keep away from them, for they are as poisonous weeds in the Church, infecting, in some way or other, all around them, and must, and will be, rooted out in due time.

These are the very bane of the Church! May God, in mercy, lessen their number daily!

Do not speak peace to a poor soul before God has spoken it. The murder of souls is the most dire of all murders! Hold in memory Ezekiel 33:7-8, "Son of man, I have made you a watchman for the house of Israel; so hear the word I speak and give them warning from Me. When I say to the wicked, 'O wicked man, you will surely die,' and you do not speak out to dissuade him from his ways, that wicked man will die for his sin, and I will hold you accountable for his blood." I wish that every man who considers he has been called of the Holy Spirit to preach the Gospel had this whole chapter written upon his heart. In your preaching separate the precious from the vile, and be ready at a moment's warning to give an account of your stewardship. Great is your responsibility! Oh, be faithful over a few things, that you may have a "Well done, good and faithful servant!" I heard a clergyman in your neighborhood say, "All that we have to do is to keep the people quiet." This man was never called of the Holy Spirit to preach Christ's Gospel. Satan is only too pleased with such. This is just as the Deceiver would have it. He would keep the people quiet in their own sins, and say, "There is no danger; it is time enough yet, for you are good enough, and have done no evil, at any rate, you are no worse than others. Peace, peace!"

What a mercy that there are better things in store for us than this poor world could give! Who that knows the truth experimentally would wish to live in this base world one moment longer than he could help it. But what must that place be which infinite love has prepared for us! "There are many rooms in My Father's home, and I am going to prepare a place for you. When everything is ready,

I will come and get you, so that you will always be with Me
where I am." Does it not appear as though Jesus could not
enjoy heaven itself to the full if all His redeemed ones were
not there? "Father, I want those you have given Me to be
with Me where I am, and to see My glory." To be with
Jesus! One moment of this is worth ten thousand worlds!

We need Jesus! We cannot do without Him! We
must have Him, for He is our joy, our exceeding joy, our
life, and our all. Without Him, the world and all it calls
good, is poverty, wretchedness, and woe! With Him, a
wilderness is a paradise, a cottage a palace, and the lowliest
spot of earth a little heaven below!

As to the subject of the study of prophecy, I would
remark that, we should keep in mind the truth that "the
testimony of Jesus is the spirit of prophecy;" and that the
prophecies should be studied with a view of knowing more
of Him; His personal glory, salvation, and kingdom. There
is great danger of being led away from the 'spirit of
prophecy.' The writings of the prophets would possess no
meaning, charm, or attraction, did they not all testify of
Jesus. "Of Him give all the prophets witness." They predict
His advent, describe His death, foretell His triumph, and
portray His kingdom and glory. The suffering and
victorious Messiah is the central object of their magnificent
picture! In the study of the prophets there is great danger of
being carried away with some favorite prophetical scheme
which, perhaps, we rather bring to, than take from, their
inspired writings. And this is allowed a too absorbing study
and attention, to the exclusion of more vital and
momentous subjects. May we not be liable to lose, in a too
exclusive and engrossing study of the prophetical writings,
much of that lowliness of mind, close intimacy with the
progress of the kingdom of God within us, and communion

with God Himself, which constitute the life and spirit of experimental religion?

Whatever others may say, I am sure there was nothing good in me to draw the Savior's love. "I will have mercy upon whom I will have mercy, and I will have compassion upon whom I will have compassion." Here is the cause! Chosen in Christ before the world began; given to Christ in the councils of eternity; called; justified; and in due time glorified when the work of sanctification shall be complete. This is the glorious mystery which keeps the poor believing sinner low at the feet of Jesus! Boasting is here excluded! A sinner saved, fully and eternally saved through the all sufficient merit and atoning blood of Christ the Lord. It is a free grace salvation! Without money, without price! No other would have saved such a sinner as me! If there had been anything necessary in me, I would have been lost to all eternity! It is a free grace salvation!

My heart feels for you, my dear friend, in your deep, deep trial. This present world is a world of sadness; but when we think of that world which is to come, into which sorrow never enters, and how soon we may be there, we may well "rejoice in tribulation." Our "light affliction, which is but for a moment, works for us a far more exceeding and eternal weight of glory." In all your sorrows, pour out your heart to the Man of sorrows. He will bow down His ear and listen to all you say, and will either remove or moderate your trial, and give you strength to bear it. Even this bitter draught He has given you to drink shall result both in your good and His own glory. Remember, not a sparrow falls upon the ground without His guidance, and that the very hairs of your head are all numbered. How much more has this trying event been ordered and arranged by Him who loves you! Infinite wisdom has appointed the whole! Never doubt that He loves you when He the most deeply afflicts. "When you go through deep waters and great trouble, I will be with you. When you go through rivers of difficulty, you will not drown! When you walk through the fire, you will not be burned up; the flames will not consume you." May He lift up upon you the light of His countenance, drawing you nearer to Himself, that you may see what a tender, loving heart He has for you, and how deeply and tenderly and considerately He cares for you, as if there were not another poor sorrowful one to care for on the face of the whole earth!

I wonder what business a man, declaring himself sent of God to lead poor sinners to Christ, has to do with the sights and shows of this perishing world! How can he exhort his flock to live above the world and all its vanities, while he himself is going after them? I cannot understand some Christians, and they do not understand me. I may be wrong; but when I read, "Come out from among them, and be separate." "Do not love the world, nor the things that are in the world;" and many other such solemn exhortations, I realize the way a believer in Christ should live, and have only to regret I so often wander from it myself. Oh, how the world, with all its cares, crowds upon the poor pilgrim, even in his most solemn moments! "Dear Savior, keep me near, very near Your blessed heart. Shelter me under Your almighty, protecting wing, until the storm of life is past."

Broad is the road to destruction, and many go therein; narrow is the road that leads to glory, and there are few, comparatively, who find it; happy few! And, oh, what a mercy that He has guided our feet there! Our souls and bodies ought to be devoted to Him, to glorify Him for His distinguishing grace! For what are we more than others, that He should fix His everlasting love upon us while we were dead in trespasses and in sins? Blessed be God, who passes by so many, and who has deigned to look upon us who were lying as others, dead in sin. Infinite in sovereignty, infinite in goodness, infinite in power! Why He passes by some and calls others is only known to Himself. But He will have mercy upon whom He will have mercy. Blessed, forever blessed, be His adored name! Oh, for grace to serve Him better, and to love Him more!

This world is not, and never was intended to be, our rest. It is a wilderness we are passing through, and shame, shame to us, that we so often want to sit down amid its weeds and briars, and amuse ourselves with the trifles of a fallen world lying in the wicked one. All here is polluted and tainted by sin; therefore does Christ say, "Arise, my love, my fair one, and come away."

We must not expect much in this base world. All our richest blessings are to come. This world is but a preparatory state. We are disciplining and preparing for the glorious inheritance above. But how often, through wretched unbelief, we seem to wish to have our all here. And although, from bitter experience, we feel and acknowledge that this poor world is polluted, and it is not our rest, yet more or less we go on, often repining, because we cannot have things just as we wish. Oh, to leave ourselves in a loving, tender Father's hands! He knows what we need, and what we ought to have, and will deny us no good thing. But He must judge for us, who are but as babes, who cannot judge for ourselves.

Oh, dear friend, the world is one vast hospital filled with diseased inmates, and only one class can ever hope for a perfect cure. We believers shall all be well when we get above. This world is not our rest, nor our home. We seek a better one, and, blessed be God, our best Friend is preparing it for us. When we get there we shall find it far beyond our highest and most enlarged expectations.

Who would desire to live aways in this poor world? Who would desire to dwell on these lower grounds, where sickness and sorrow, the sad consequences of sin, follow in our wake? In heaven, our happy home, we shall enjoy perfect holiness and perfect happiness.

Is it not strange that we can for one moment lose sight of heaven, and the increasing glory, and grovel in the dust to gather pebbles, for the pleasure of throwing them afterwards away?

What a mercy of mercies that He has condescended to call us out of darkness into His marvellous light, and to translate us into the kingdom of His dear Son! What do we not owe Him for this rich display of sovereign mercy? I often have to exclaim, "Lord, why me? Why such a poor sinner as I am, to be brought near unto God, adopted into His family, made an heir of God, and a joint heir with Christ Jesus?"

Who can subdue sin in us but Jesus? I might as well attempt to remove mountains as to reason away one corruption of my fallen nature. But if we, the moment we detect it, carry it to Jesus, He will do it all for us. This is one of the most difficult lessons to learn in the school of Christ. I am but just beginning to learn it, and therefore I am placed in the youngest class, traveling to Jesus more as a little helpless child, for Him to do all for and all in me. My imagined strength is all vanished, my boasted reason turned into folly, and now, thus living on Christ in childlike simplicity, my peace, joy, and consolation are past expression. Oh, the love, the matchless love of Jesus to a poor sinner lying thus at His dear feet, waiting to receive a welcoming smile beaming from His countenance. Dear friend, keep close to Him. Let not the world or its cares come between you and Christ.

What a difficult matter it is to be in the world, and yet not to be of the world! Our Lord Himself carried out this principle. He passed through the world as one who was not of it. Oh, that we could but imitate His holy example, and aim only, while in it, so to let our light shine, that others may take knowledge of us that we have been with Jesus, and have learned of Him. It should be our whole endeavor to do all the good we can in it and for it; and yet to set at nothing its spirit, its principles, and its maxims. How can a believer walk through this world safely and securely? Only as he is upheld by a strength that is Omnipotent! I am passing through a world lying in the wicked one. I belong to another kingdom, which is not of this world. Dear friend, see, then, your high calling! He has called you to come out of the world and to be separate; in principle, in practice, in heart.

What a brittle thing is all the glory, wealth, and honor of this vain world! How empty, and what trash does it appear! And yet men sell their souls to grasp it, and at last pass away from it and find it all a phantom. How unceasing is Satan in forever bringing it before our eyes, in some form or other! What is all the pomp and wealth and rank of this poor fleeting world, in contrast with the glory that shall soon be revealed in all those who love His appearing?

When disappointed in the creature, I take refuge at once in Jesus. I run to Him, and find Him all my heart could wish. "Lord, how could I live without You? You are my all in all, my comfort, my joy, my peace, my strengthener, my home for time and eternity! Helpless as an infant I hang upon You!"

How wonderful is God in all His great and gracious dealings. He places us, as soon as the spiritual eye is opened, in His school. First, the infant school; and then onward and upward, from class to class, losing no opportunity of spiritual instruction. Many hard lessons have we to learn and to relearn. But, oh, the unwearied patience and tenderness of our Teacher! Some of His children are slow learners, dull scholars, and require the discipline of the rod to stimulate them to more earnestness, attention, and submission. Some imagine they have arrived at the end of their education, and sit down at their ease; but presently they are called upon to solve some hard problem, and they find that they know less than they thought, and for their boasting are sent back to a lower class, and made to commence where they first began. Such is the school of Christ.

"Lord, teach me more and more of Yourself, and of my own poverty, misery, and weakness. And oh, unfold to my longing eyes and heart what there is in Yourself to supply all my need, and in Your loving, willing heart, to do all for me, and all in me, to fit me for Your service here, and for your presence hereafter! Sanctify abundantly all Your varying dispensations to the welfare and prosperity of my soul, and increase in me every gift and grace of Your Spirit, that I may show forth Your praise, and walk humbly and closely with You. You know what a poor, worthless worm I am, and how utterly unworthy of the least mercy from Your merciful hands; but You love to bestow Your favors upon the poor and needy, such as me, most precious Lord. You have been a good and gracious, sin pardoning God to my soul, and a very present help in every time of trouble. Leave me not, nor forsake me, now that old age is overtaking me, and grey hairs thicken upon me. I know You will not. You, who have been with me all my journey, will not leave me now; for You are faithful who has promised. I feel my dependence on You more than ever. Without You I can do nothing. Helpless as an infant I hang upon You, to do all for me and all in me."

We are hastening fast through time. Time is short, and eternity, with all its solemn realities, is before us. What is our life? How uncertain! and yet is it not awfully true that poor wretched man rushes heedlessly on, thoughtless of what awaits him in an endless eternity? We are traveling fast through this wilderness world, and soon shall pass away. Let us, then, feel more like pilgrims and strangers here. Let us not seek our rest where our precious Jesus had no place to lay His head. Let us rejoice more in the prospect of that glorious inheritance prepared for us above, where He is who has loved us unto the death. Oh, for ten thousand worlds would I not have my portion here in this wilderness!

The believer's life is changeful and chequered. The path along which he is retracing his steps back to paradise is paved with stones of variegated hues. And yet, painfully diversified as are often the events in his history, that very diversity is as essential to the symmetry and completeness of his Christian character as are different shades of coloring to the perfection of a picture, or as opposite notes in music are to the creation of harmony.

Avoid light, trifling professors of religion; their influence will be as poison to your souls. I am convinced that much communion with lukewarm professors does great injury to the believer. Oh, avoid such! Light and trifling conversation acts as a poison to the life of God in the soul. It grieves the Spirit, and He withdraws His sensible influence.

If the religion of Christ does not make us happy, nothing else will. But the happiness of the believer is very different from that of the world. It arises from a sublimer source, and shuts out unwholesome levity and mirth. The highest state of enjoyment here below, which can arise from a believing view of Him who was pierced for our sins and wounded for our transgressions, will ever be accompanied with the humble and contrite heart; a deep sense of our rebellion before conversion, and of our ingratitude and unprofitableness since. So here is joy, yet mixed with sorrow. This is happiness the world knows nothing of. Be assured I am happy, and do rejoice in God, while I often have occasion to sigh at what I feel within, and at what I behold around me.

Sin darkens the eye and hardens the heart.

Realize more and more your glorious inheritance, and do not covet the poor trifles of time and sense.

In heaven I will see my own most precious Redeemer, enthroned in all His glory, His countenance radiant with ineffable love, and a welcome beaming from every feature. So shall I behold Him who loved me with an everlasting love and landed me at last in the kingdom of glory. The redeemed shall all be encircling the throne, and basking in the full sunshine of the Redeemer's countenance;

while I shall lie prostrate at His feet in wondering joy and adoring love at the matchless grace that brought me there.

When Christians meet together, they talk too much about religion, preachers, and sermons. I cannot but think, that if they communed less about religion, and more of Jesus, it would give a higher tone of spirituality to their conversation, and prove more refreshing to the soul. He would then oftener draw near, and make Himself one in their midst, and talk with them by the way.

God be praised for His wondrous goodness to me, as poor and needy a sinner as ever lived; and yet I shall live forever, and rejoice in God my Savior through an endless eternity!

"Lord, here is my heart, my poor heart. Take it just as it is, and make it all that You would have it to be; cast it into Your mold, and let it receive and reflect Your image, Son of God, inexpressibly precious Jesus, Savior of sinners, Redeemer of my never dying soul!"

Jesus is the Fountain, yes, the Ocean, of living waters. We draw supplies from His infinite, inexhaustible fulness. "Lord, impart to me more of Yourself. Fill this heart with Your love, engrave Your image there, and let me not lose sight of You for one small moment."

Jesus is all in all to me. I feel a blessed nearness to Him, to heaven. My soul holds converse with Him, and sweet I find it to lie as a helpless infant at His feet; yes, passive in His loving hands, knowing no will but His.

What a mercy, thus to unburden the whole heart; the tried and weary, the tempted and sorrowful heart; tried

by sin, tried by Satan, tried by those you love! What a
mercy to have a loving bosom to flee to, one truly loving
heart to confide in, which responds to the faintest breathing
of the Spirit! "Precious Jesus, how inexpressibly dear are
You to me at this moment! Keep sensibly near to me. Lift
up upon me Your heavenly countenance, for it is sweeter,
dearer, better than life!"

Vast as eternity are His mercies, infinite His
perfections, and wonderful all His ways. What will eternity
disclose to my astonished sight, my eyes then unveiled to
see what now I understand not!

I shall soon exchange earth for heaven, and finally
close my eyes, when I shall re-open them in glory. Oh, to
be there! Oh, to see Jesus face to face! To behold Him
whom my soul loves, and be with Him forever! But a little
while, and I am there!

My sins, which are mountains high, are all
pardoned, blotted out of the book of God's remembrance by
the precious blood of His dear and well beloved Son. Praise
God for His marvellous goodness to me a sinner!

What a blessing it is to have such a Friend to go to
as Jesus, with all our difficulties, small and great,
transferring them to His hands who is infinite in wisdom
and in power, and will do all things well. Is not this a
mercy worth recording in letters of gold, to be written in
the deep recesses of every believing heart?

Without Jesus life would be an aching void, earth a
wilderness of woe and sorrow! He can transform this
wilderness into a little heaven, making it radiant with His
presence! What must heaven itself be!

No weeping in heaven! Blessed be God for the hope He has given us beyond this scene of sin and sorrow. Let us arise, and travel on!

I think, if I had ten thousand hearts, I would give them all to Jesus!

I am increasingly persuaded that it is alone by constant communion with Jesus, that we can attain to any progression in the divine life.

No happiness that all the glory of this world could produce is equal to that of a broken heart at the feet of Jesus. It is sweet to creep into the very bosom of Christ, while we feel how utterly worthless and unworthy, yet how welcome, we are.

His will is best at all times. For the world, I would not be left to have my own way in any one thing.

Prayer brings heaven down into the soul, and lifts the soul towards heaven.

Let us live more for eternity, and less for this poor dying world.

For wise and gracious purposes, the Lord chastens those whom He loves. Let us lie passive in His hands, leaving ourselves to be dealt with according to His infinite wisdom and love. I know you have your cares; but if you would carry them simply to Christ, He would make the rough places plain and the crooked straight. In every difficulty go at once to Jesus, before you decide in your own mind, or listen to the dictates of your own heart. Jesus so loves you, that He would not lay the weight of a feather upon you more than is needful.

Dear friend, let us live more decidedly for a glorious eternity. We are here but for a little while, and then pass away. A crown of glory awaits the poor sinner who clings to Jesus. I hope to meet you in that better world to which we are all so rapidly approaching.

Pray, pray, pray without ceasing! God listens to your faintest breathing.

So eternal and deep, so sovereign and boundless is the love of God, that angels cannot fathom it! He is nothing but unfeigned, constant, and unabating love, to the weakest, the most unworthy of all His little flock.

Oh, the goodness of God, the wonders of His matchless love! Eternity will be only long enough to tell of it.

My dear friend, have constant transactions with your precious Savior. A holy familiarity with Him will tend much to conform to His likeness. This simple living upon Christ has a most sanctifying, purifying tendency upon the whole inner man; and thus sin grows more hateful, and the world less attractive, and the pleasures of sense increasingly distasteful, and we are better fitted to sustain the trials of life.

Oh, dear friend, let us often meditate on heaven; it will assist us to bear more serenely the ills of life.

Oh, the wondrous love of God in the gift of His beloved Son, to suffer, bleed, and die for such poor, wretched sinners!

Oh, think of lost souls, of the eternal woe, where the worm dies not, and the fire is not quenched! Let us put far from us all the false charity that leaves sinners to stand upon the precipice of hell, because we will not disturb their carnal security.

Godly parents cannot convert their children; God alone can do this. But they can lead them to Jesus, and bring them up in the fear of the Lord. And when they have done this, they have done all they can do; for the Holy Spirit alone can change the heart. They must be born again. Christ has said it. The new birth is not a change of sentiment, nor an outward reformation of life; it is a new heart implanted by the Holy Spirit.

How many are wasting their precious time on the things of this poor world they are so soon to leave, and are risking the never dying soul, yet hastening on to the judgement of God, unprepared for that great day for which all other days were made! Is not this madness?

Bless God with me, that we are both so near our home, each day's travel bringing us nearer and nearer. Our eyes shall behold Him whom our souls love beyond all created good. What a prospect is before us! Forever with the Lord! Our journey is drawing to an end. Look forward, look upward. Jesus's eye is upon you; His heart is towards you. A few more severe trials, a few more staggering steps, and we are there!

What a heart has Christ! Do you know what it is made of? It is an ocean of goodness. It is a sea, fathomless and shoreless, of matchless love; love to poor sinners, who but look to Him or sigh for Him. One loving look from Christ will dissolve your heart into love and sweet contrition.

Oh, to have such a Friend as Jesus, who feels all our sorrows, carries all our burdens, and has promised to bring us safely through this trying world, and place us at last at His own right hand, where neither sickness nor sorrow shall ever come!

"If you love Me, keep My commandments." Not one nor two only, but all. It is not given us to choose which we shall keep, and which we shall break.

I am looking heavenward. There is my only, my best Friend, and there is my heart. Behold Him seated on His throne, and all the goodly company of the redeemed around Him. Oh, the blessedness of beholding all His unveiled beauties, and of basking in the sunshine of His countenance! Does not your heart burn within you when you think of these things, these glorious realities? Well, beloved, we shall all soon see Him eye to eye, face to face. There is much of heaven to be enjoyed while here, a foretaste of what we shall realize through eternity.

Christ has been with you in all your late deep trial, and He is with you now. See what a Friend you have by your side; to talk to in your solitude; to tell Him all you feel and fear, all you wish and need! Oh, what a Friend is Jesus! He is better than ten thousand husbands or children. What a Friend has He been to worthless me! I could not live without Him here, nor in heaven either. He is the chief of all my joys, and my comfort by day and by night.

This life is a dark passage to a world of light and glory above.

Beloved fellow traveler in the kingdom of God, it is through much tribulation we are to enter into His kingdom of glory above. I have heard of the severe trial your Father has sent in much love. When we arrive at home, and trace our steps through this wilderness, we shall see that every trial, cross, and disappointment was needful, and that the work would not have been complete without all, even the least. Our loving God and Father takes no pleasure in afflicting us; but it is by these things we are brought to be better acquainted with ourselves and with Him. He does it all. Can anything happen to us but what God does in love to our souls? Are we not in His heart, and can anything happen to us but what He designs? Cast all your cares on Him, for He cares for you. He is better able to bear the burden than you are. Lie contented in His loving hands, and let Him take His own way with you.

Yes, beloved, even your present trial shall be to the praise of His dear and holy name. Be of good cheer! God has commissioned it as a messenger of love, nothing but love; eternal, never ending love! Only trust Him for all consequences. He is doing all things well. Leave yourself in His blessed hands, and seek more for cheerful submission than for the removal of the trial. Be earnest for submission, and He will give it, and resignation will follow, and then what a calm! Be quiet in His hands, and feel that His will must be best, because He is God, and knows the end from the beginning, while we know nothing! I would not now have been without my trial for a thousand worlds. Oh, the goodness of God! His name is love, and wondrous is He in all His dealings with us; and He is dealing with us every moment of our brief existence. May the Lord comfort and guide you in every step you take, and enable you to repose passive in His dear hands, is the prayer of your affectionate sister in a precious Jesus.

The rod, our all wise Father will not withhold. And what a mercy it is to be able to bear the rod, and to see the cause! But how often do we close our ears, and go on in our crooked way until He speaks by some louder and yet heavier blow! And then it is our mercy to run at once into the tender, loving bosom of God, confess our sin, and beg for renewed grace, to enable us to forsake it.

Fallen human nature sometimes puts on a show of religion, and will go a great way while the heart is not changed, and the fear of God and the love of the Spirit is not there, and is not known. Thousands, I fear, deceive themselves with this resemblance of true religion.

Oh to have the heart right with God! It is so awfully deceitful, and we are so continually more or less deceived by it, that we imagine all is right, when, in fact, all may be wrong.

The oftener the gold is put into the furnace, the more the dross is consumed, and the brighter it shines. In our trials, we cling closer to Jesus; we see more of his loving heart, and imbibe more of His holy image.

The way the Lord is teaching you is the right way. To be well acquainted with our own hearts is to bring us nearer to Jesus, and to make us more firmly cling to the cross. Your poor heart is the same as it was years ago, but there was no light to show its evil. But as you grow in grace you will see more and more the goodness of God in the gift of His dear Son, to make an all sufficient atonement for sinners so vile and utterly helpless as we are. It is a great mercy that, while the Holy Spirit opens up the deep fountain of iniquity within our hearts to our view, He also, at the same time, shows us the Fountain open, always open, in which we may wash and be clean. This makes Jesus so precious to the deeply taught Christian.

Oh, God is such an ocean of love to me! The more His wondrous love is manifested, the more I hate and abhor myself!

Oh, how strange that God should listen, and so listen, as if he said, "Yes, yes!" to every request I make! He overcomes me with His love. He breaks my heart, then heals it again. It is His love that does it. He gives godly sorrow; puts forth His hand and draws me near to Himself, and then says, What is your petition, and what is your request? Then I hasten to tell Him all, all, as if I feared He would withdraw before I could do so. But He lingers and listens, and then sends me away rejoicing that I have such a Friend in heaven, and longing to drop this body of sin and death, that I might be with Him.

Oh, the matchless love that is in our reconciled Father's heart? Can we suppose for a moment that He sees not our trials, temptations, and conflicts; and that He is not caring for, and watching over us? Oh, no; God is with us and for us, working all things, even now, for our good and His glory!

How wearisome is the poor body, creeping to the grave! It is a dying body, but it shall rise again!

Look at the scenes of a busy world, how they pass away! It is but as the buzzing of a summer fly, and all is gone. Therefore, set your affections on things above!

What a mercy to have a good and gracious God to look to, and ask what you will, and to know that He always hears and stands ready to answer! Think what an honor put upon a poor worm, to have the ear and the heart of the mighty God! To know that He loves you, and cannot cease to love, because He cannot change. He knows what we were, and what we would be to the end; and yet He loved us, and will love throughout eternity! And what does He require? Only our heart, just as it is, with all its imperfections.

What is the world, or the glory of a thousand such perishing worlds as this, when compared with the glory that shall be revealed in those who love His appearing?

Oh, what a God we have to do with! so full of love and compassion; and although He tries us, it is all in love, to bring us to know Him more, that we might love Him better.

My heart is often overwhelmed at the thought of His avowing such a worthless worm as myself as one of His sheep for whom He shed His precious blood. Dear friend, let us never for a moment forget what we were, and what we now are!

Let us aim to walk humbly and confidingly with Jesus, and never allow Him to be out of our sight. Oh, to travel on, leaning upon our Beloved! His arm will support us in our feebleness; His eye will guide us in our blindness; He will strengthen, uphold, and comfort us, and never leave nor forsake us. May the Lord bless you with much of His sensible presence; and when we get above, we will unite our praises to Him who has loved us, and washed us in His own most precious blood!

Oh, the infinite value of a throne of grace! There is an enjoyment in communion with the holy God, of which the worldling knows nothing. It is foolishness with the wisest of men; but the sincere, lowly follower of Christ Jesus, loved by God, regenerated by the Holy Spirit, is made to sit in heavenly places in Christ Jesus.

The atmosphere of heaven is love. When we arrive there, we shall swim in an ocean of love!

It is a happy position for a believer to be in, when he is brought to that point to see he can do nothing for himself, then to rest and wait patiently for the Lord, fully believing He will do all things in the best possible way. Whatever the Lord does in this way for us, is the best, the very best; better than with all our wisdom and management we could have done for ourselves. I am persuaded, the more we live by faith the holier and the happier we are. Is it not written, Cast all your care upon Him, for He cares for you? Why, then, need I be anxious, when my Savior is caring for me? Are not my concerns His concerns, and has He ever failed me? Then, oh my soul, why not trust Him now?

What a suffering world is this! What a mercy to be able to look beyond this dying world, to the prospect of meeting Him who has pardoned all my transgressions, and of being with Him forever! And shall I, the unworthiest of the unworthy, see Him face to face, against whom I have so often sinned, whose Spirit I have so often grieved? Shall I be near Him, and be permitted to love Him as my soul wishes now to do, but cannot? Oh, glorious prospect! My heart is humbled while I rejoice in the wondrous goodness of a sin pardoning God, who could, and does, love such a one as I. How I long to be holy even as He is holy! And will it not be so? When I drop this vile body, shall I not awake in His righteousness? When I see Him, shall I not be like Him?

Let it be our chief aim to glorify Jesus, to live upon Him, and live for Him. Oh, He is most precious, so tender, so full of love, so watchful over our interests, caring for us in all things, and entering into all our poor concerns!

What a constant source of temptation the world is, in some shape or other, to the believer all through his journey homeward! Its cares and its pursuits, its pleasures and its claims, lawful though they be, yet, through the weakness of the flesh, are a constant snare to the heavenly pilgrim! Its principles and its spirit are adverse to the prosperity of the soul, which struggles on through a host of foes. "Precious Jesus, strengthen Your poor dust, and enable me to cling closer and closer to You."

At times my heart is overwhelmed with a sense of His unmerited love towards one so utterly unworthy. I long to be with Him. The thought of heaven is very sweet. I long to see Him in glory who has so frequently and tenderly dealt with me.

Live much in heaven, and earth will grow less attractive.

Whatever draws or drives us to Jesus is good. The oftener we go the better. The Lord frequently places us in such peculiar circumstances as compel us to apply to Him for the help we can get nowhere else. May the Lord enable us more and more to look alone to Him, for He is a present help in every time of need. His heart overflows with tenderness, sympathy, and love.

It is good to feel that we are in the Lord's hands, and that all our trials, small and great, are designed by Him for the furthering His work in our souls. They are great blessings in disguise to a child of God. Nothing takes place, within or without, but is designed for our especial benefit and the glory of His own dear name. We shall have to thank Him for all when we see Him face to face. What a blessed time will that be! How much do we need of weaning from this poor disappointing world; a world lying in the wicked one; and yet so closely do we cling to it. He who loves us is compelled to give us many a wrench to tear us from it. Love not the world, neither the things that are in the world.

PART 2:

"Jesus, You are my chief joy, my life, my all.
Without You this world would be wretchedness itself.
Keep, oh keep me near Yourself, nearer, nearer still; and
allow no earthly love to occupy Your place in my heart."

All events are in His hands to direct, and overrule,
and bless to His own redeemed people.

When a corrupted Christianity spreads, what cold,
heartless formality prevails!

What communion can a formalist have with God?
Communion is supposed to be an interchange of sentiment,
feeling, and expression. What communion could one have
with a statue? You may speak to it, question it; but there is
no response, no intimation of feeling, no communion. So is
it with the mere religious formalist. He regularly says his
prayers, but it is to an unknown God. He repeats the same
again and again, but he does not know the Being he
addresses. There is no response, no interchange of feeling;
above all, of love. There is no answer from the Lord, no
bending down of His ear, no lifting up of His countenance,
no cheering welcome. Sadly, the formalist is satisfied with
this. He does what he thinks is his duty. He repeats his
lifeless, heartless prayers, and thinks he has done well. And
so he lives and dies with a lie in his right hand, unless God,
in His sovereign mercy, awakens him from his awful
delusion, and shows him his lost and undone condition.

Go with all you need to Jesus; keep nothing back.
Go with all the simplicity of a babe, and tell Jesus. He will
bow down His loving ear, and listen to all you have to say
to Him.

Oh, let us bow our neck to the cross, for Jesus is walking with us every step of the way! When tried, rush at once into the very bosom of Christ, and feel the warm pulsations of His own loving heart, and rest your head there. All will be well. He is with you now, and will never leave nor forsake you.

Oh, the wondrous, the ocean like love of Jesus! Who can fathom it?

Oh, carry all your needs to Him, not doubting that He not only hears you, but is every moment watching over you! All is well, and though dark clouds come between, there is a bright light behind them. Go at once with your trouble, be it what it may; nothing is too trivial to carry to Him. Let us come to Jesus and bring to Him all our cares, large and small, and tell Him all that is in our hearts.

Oh, the care of the Good Shepherd! His wakeful eye is ever upon us, and His loving heart is ever towards us!

In heaven we shall have new bodies, more beauteous than the brightest angel in heaven, and standing, too, nearer to the Savior than they.

Oh, we shall see, when we arrive in heaven, how wonderful has been the wisdom that has guided us in all our journey through! You may be quite certain that all that takes place, small or great, is in that covenant that is ordered in all things and sure. Nothing is uncertain with God. A sparrow falls not to the ground without Him. You are of more value than many sparrows.

Jesus is indeed very precious to my soul. All creature love sinks into nothing before it. The more I see of the fulness, the boundless love of Christ, the more I sink in the dust of self abasement before Him.

What could we do in this world of manifold temptations, had we not a God to go to, ever ready to be a present help?

Allow no distance to arise between you and your best Friend. He has undertaken for us in all things. We need Him as our Counselor, as our Guide, as our Protector, as our Deliverer, in ten thousand ways. How needful and how sweet to be ever sitting at His feet, looking up and meeting His eye bending down upon us in love!

Confession of sin is one of the most sweet, holy, and profitable exercises of the soul. It endears us to Christ, and endears Christ to us. It brings us into a brokenhearted, contrite communion with a loving, sympathizing Savior, purifies the heart, and keeps the conscience tender and watchful.

Death, to the believer, is but passing out of a world of sorrow and of sin, and entering upon a world of indescribable glory! If we lived more in anticipation of the happiness that waits us, earth would have less hold on our hearts' best affections.

All His dispensations are designed to draw you closer to Himself, and He would remove every object that comes between Him and you. You shall not have one trial too much. His loving eye is upon you; let yours be upon Him.

Dear friend, keep close to Jesus, and the throne of grace. If you feel your heart cold, go at once, and He will warm it. If you feel it hard and impenitent, go, and He will soften and awaken it to sweet contrition. Go, under all circumstances and with all frames. All your difficulties, however small or however great, you have a right to bring to Jesus, casting all your care upon Him, for He cares for you. Dear friend, we need to live more upon Him, like little helpless children. May the Lord bless and keep you very near Himself, is the prayer of your sincere friend in Christ.

It was love, infinite love that brought Jesus down to earth. It was love, infinite love that led Him to pass through the tremendous conflict, when he grappled with death, hell, and the grave. It was love, infinite love that sustained Him in it, and that brought Him out of it a royal Conqueror. It was love, infinite love that bore Him back to heaven, where He is now, and where we shall be also. And now, what have we to do here, but to glorify Him who has done such great things for us?

Oh the glorious prospect that is before the feeblest child of God! Look often at your inheritance. Take your walks in the 'garden of love' above! See Jesus there, no longer wearing a crown of thorns, but a diadem of glory!

Let us ever trust Jesus for His unchanging and unchangeable love. From everlasting to everlasting He has loved us; and all the varying dispensations of His loving providence are only to prepare us more completely for the place He is now preparing for us. Let us aim to see Him in all things, and to have Him ever present with us. How sweet to walk through this wilderness with our hand in His hand, feeling that He is leading us safely along the narrow road that leads to everlasting life. Dear friend, may Jesus be more and more precious to you and I. None but Jesus can make us happy here and hereafter.

Join me in praising God for His great and distinguishing mercy to us, in opening our eyes, and leading us to His beloved Son, that we might be saved, with a sure and everlasting salvation.

How is it with your soul? Are your prospects growing brighter and brighter as you travel on? Do you find Jesus nearer and more precious day by day? What progress have you made? You have had your conflicts, your wanderings, and backslidings many; but still onwards you must go. There is no standstill in this journey. Tell me when you saw Him last, and how you feel in the prospect of soon being with the beloved One forever and ever. I am not happy here without Him, and would be miserable indeed, were I not quite sure of seeing and dwelling with Him in glory. Jesus is all in all to my soul, and life would be wearisome indeed were it not so. He makes up the sum of my happiness here, and will be my joy, my life, and my glory hereafter. Dear friend, let us speed more our journey, nor loiter in the way.

Oh that the saints of God would live more in the anticipation of the glory that awaits them! There is much of heaven to be enjoyed even on earth. Let us live, too, more in holy familiarity with Jesus. Nothing is too much beneath His notice.

Jesus is the very same Jesus now that He was when He walked the streets of Jerusalem. Though His body is glorified, He is not altered. His heart is still the same, full of sympathy and love, ready to listen to all we have to say to Him, and to do all we ask Him to do, and in the best possible way. Precious Jesus! Is He not altogether lovely? He is everything to my soul. Life would be an aching void without Him.

Oh, how few really know God! I meet with many hearsay Christians, who have heard of Jesus, as Job did, with the hearing of the ear, but who have no personal acquaintance with Him. They have never come to Christ as poor, wretched, blind, and naked; and therefore they know nothing of that peace which the application of the atoning blood alone can impart. They have never come in contact with Christ. They only believe what others say of Him, and know nothing of a blessed recognition, a oneness and a holy communion between Jesus and the poor sinner, saved by sovereign grace, and eternal, everlasting love.

Oh, the luxury of prayer! To have true communion, familiar communion with God. To talk with God! To go and shut the door, and tell God all, all that is in our heart! To feel that He is listening to hear what we have to say to Him; and then to wait and see what He will say to us! No tongue can tell the rich enjoyment of sitting in all the helplessness of an infant at His feet, and know that He is listening to all I say to Him. I rest on His loving, fatherly care!

What could we do in this poor dying world without a throne of grace, and a God of grace upon the throne, in our every time of need? Oh, let us keep close to Him who loved us with an everlasting love, and with loving kindness has drawn us to Himself.

We are journeying to the inheritance which the Lord our God has given to us, through a world crowded with temptations on either side, which would divert us from the way, if it were possible. Our worst foe, the body of sin and of death, we bear about with us. But our Jesus is for us, and we can say, "More are they who are for us, than they who are against us."

We are traveling fast, and at every step are nearing
our heavenly home! We shall see Jesus soon! Oh, how
soon! Jesus sits, in all the majesty of heaven, waiting to
welcome His pilgrims home.

May you be led to see unceasingly that this world is
not worthy of one anxious thought! It is all passing away,
and we shall soon stand before the great white throne!

We are on a race course. The point from which we
start is conversion; the goal to which we run is heaven; the
prize for which we contend is a crown of glory, which the
righteous Judge will give us at that great day. If, dear
friend, you have started in this race, so run that you may
obtain. Go forward. Do not rest where you are. How few
lay these great things to heart! The world and its trifles so
engross the thoughts, that God, and Christ, and eternity,
with our vast responsibility, are shut out of sight; and
Satan, the great foe of mankind, gains his point, unless
sovereign grace interferes, and opens the blind eye to see
the danger, and Jesus the Refuge!

Oh, it is with a holy, heart searching God that we
have to do. And the soul is of more value than ten million
worlds. What shall it profit a man if he gain the whole
world and lose his own soul? These are solemn, awful
truths; but only by a few are they laid to heart.

None will ever come to Jesus until they feel that
they are lost and undone in themselves. He came not to call
the righteous, but sinners to repentance.

Oh, what is all the grandeur, wealth, and honor of
this fleeting world, compared with the glory that awaits the
believer in Jesus? Kings and queens pass away, and leave

their crowns; but the Christian goes to his, and wears it through eternity, ever bright, ever pure!

How much more are our thoughts engaged with this present evil world, and our poor decaying bodies, than concerned to know what awaits us in an endless eternity. Is not this one of Satan's devices? He will endeavor to often engage our thoughts with inconsequential trifles that would shame a child, in order to hide from us the eternal realities of the glory that awaits the believer. Oh, let us beware of Satan's devices!

We cannot utter one real prayer but by the Holy Spirit. He it is who shows us our iniquity and helplessness, teaches us how to pray and what to ask for, and then responds to our prayer.

Eternity, eternity, with all its solemn realities, is before us!

Oh, the change from earth to heaven! The thought of seeing Jesus face to face! Think, the joy of that moment!

With all its hopes and glory, this is but a poor world, even if we could possess the whole of it. Take this world in its best attire, it is but a wilderness of 'bitter sweets'.

Let us set out afresh to run the heavenly race; warmed with the love of Christ in our heart, anointed with the Holy Spirit, heaven in view, a crown of glory awaiting us, and Jesus on the throne ready to bid us welcome!

There is none on earth or in heaven like Jesus! He is the chief among ten thousand, the altogether lovely one.

Oh, love Him! Give your whole, your undivided heart to Him. If I had a thousand, He would have them all.

If your heart appears cold, hard, and insensible, take it to Jesus, and tell Him how it is with you. He will warm, soften, and fill it with His love. Go, under all circumstances, and tell Him all you feel, and all you do not feel. Let nothing come between you and your best Friend. In all your fears, failures, and discouragements, go to Him, and tell Him all.

How boundless is the love of God to the feeblest of His little ones!

What will heaven be!

Nothing so keeps the heart right as having constant communication with Christ.

I am nearing day by day my heavenly inheritance. It seems at times almost in view. It is but a step, and I am there! The more I see of Jesus, the more He opens to me His loving heart, the deeper is my sorrow for sin. I lie down in the dust of His feet closer than ever I did before. I can truly say I abhor myself in dust and ashes before Him.

My heart seems ready to melt into contrition in view of the ten thousand thousand sins, wilful and aggravating, that I have committed against Him, who loved me with an everlasting love, and with loving kindness drew me to Himself.

It is sweet to think how soon, how very soon, we shall be fitted for the companionship of Jesus Himself, beholding Him in all His unveiled beauties. Does not the thought often gladden our heart, and fill your eyes with tears of joy, and holy contrition for sin? I cannot conceive of holy joy unaccompanied with godly sorrow. Confession of sin should make up one half of our lives. Only acknowledge your iniquity. And when we remember that we have to do with One so willing and so able to pardon, it becomes then a mingled feeling of pleasure and pain. By confessing sin we gather strength to resist it; thereby the enemy of our souls is foiled, the conscience is kept tender, the heart is sanctified, and the blood of Jesus becomes increasingly precious. Let us constantly flee to the cleansing fountain!

Oh, what a pleasant prospect is before us, almost in full view! Jesus is at hand, and if He does not soon come to us, we shall soon go to Him, our best and dearest Friend. Oh, to see His face, once so wearied and careworn, traced with sorrow and with grief; and that because our sins were laid upon Him. But now resplendent with glory; His countenance is beaming with ineffable delight upon His redeemed, blood bought family, rescued from the power of hell, death, and the grave. Can we conceive of anything to equal such a scene? The Bridegroom rejoicing over his bride, saints singing, angels admiring. Endeavor to realize this, dear friend. Take your walks in the good land, flowing with milk and honey.

A throne of grace, with a broken heart for sin, and a pardoning Savior, is a verdant spot in this wilderness! Nothing in this fading world can equal it!

The more we have to do with Christ, the more we shall know of His excellences, His sympathy, and His exquisite, boundless love! May we not be satisfied to know Jesus in theory only, but in our soul's sweet experience.

There is no uncertainty with God. His thoughts of love towards us have been from everlasting to everlasting. He loved us when we were wandering far from Him, and far from happiness. He loved us when we knew Him not. He loved us out of Satan's kingdom into the kingdom of grace, and He will love us into the kingdom of glory. Our doubts and fears may harass us, but they can make no alteration in His eternal purposes.

Precious friend, look fully at Jesus. Look no longer to your own weak, sinful heart. We are to look for comfort only to Christ. The bitten Israelites looked at once and directly to the brazen serpent, and were healed. Oh the precious fountain for sin and uncleanness! I am obliged to come again and again to it.

I am fighting on my way, often sorrowing and rejoicing at the same time; mourning for my sins, while I can and do rejoice that Christ has made an all sufficient atonement for all my sins; past, present, and to come; which, while it humbles me in the dust of self abhorrence, makes me increasingly long to be like Him.

We have but a brief space left to show our love to Christ. Let us work for Him, live for Him, live to Him, and look forward to living with Him.

I would like to hear if all is well with you, and if you are making progress heavenward, homeward, and if Jesus is increasingly precious to your soul.

We do not know how soon we may be called to render in an account to God? One step and we are there, in the very presence of a holy, heart searching Jehovah. Is there anything upon earth of equal importance to this?

Worldly prosperity is unfavorable soil for the true Christian to grow in. It stupefies the soul.

What a grief it is to me to see those professing Christ, and yet living for the world. Oh that this evil might be subdued in me!

Why should our grace droop, and languish, and die, when we can repair to the Fountain of living water, at all times and under all circumstances? Oh, the blessing of having such an Almighty Friend in glory, waiting to be gracious to us, whose power is infinite in heaven and on earth; and whose love, like Himself, is from everlasting to everlasting!

True religion is essentially experimental in its nature. True Christianity is nothing less than the life of Jesus dwelling in the soul of the believer. But Christian experience varies; it may be more strongly developed in some individuals than in others. One believer may present a more robust type of this essential Christianity than another.

What, oh what shall I render unto You for Your wondrous goodness and patience towards me? Nothing have I to render. I am poor and needy, and dependent upon You moment by moment.

How intricate is often the believer's way! So hedged up that he cannot discern a single step before him. All is dark. He here and there goes too often to the creature for counsel, and perhaps for sympathy, but finds all broken cisterns. But Jesus is at hand; a Fountain of living waters, ever ready to impart all comfort, wisdom, and direction. But, oh, how slow to approach this Fountain! How base and ungrateful the heart, and wretched the unbelief that still lurks within, ever leading us away from Him who is a present help in every time of need. Take up your rest, O my soul, in Him who has loved you with an everlasting love, and will love you unto the end!

Surely I have seen an end of all perfection, both in myself and in others. But, oh, there is One, and only one, and He is perfect. The goodness, the patience, the loving kindness of Jesus surpasses our conceptions! Eternity only can unfold it to us, and we shall be even there learning it out forever and ever!

We must go in all our helplessness to Him who has said, "Without Me you can do nothing." We must cast ourselves at the feet of Him who is watching over us with a loving, sleepless eye!

The Lord has tried you of late, and I do feel anxious to speak a word of comfort to you in this affliction. Those whom He loves He invariably tries. The graces of the Spirit are thus brought into holy exercise. Jesus is thereby honored, and our souls ascend a higher round in that ladder that reaches from earth to heaven. We must sit at His feet, and believe that He does all things well. What we don't know now, we shall know hereafter. The Judge of all the earth must do right. Soon we pass away to our heavenly inheritance, and then we shall see all the way He led us through the wilderness was the right way, and that not one trial or cross could have been dispensed with. Oh, let us cling closer and closer to Him than ever. Let us make Him our all in all. May the constraining love of Christ, the eternal love of the Father, and the sanctifying love of the Holy Spirit, rest upon you, guide, and bless you!

I am near my eternal home. Jesus is very precious, and His presence is sensibly with me. I live now more as a little helpless infant upon Christ, than ever I did in my long life.

Dear friend, this is our season for the trial of faith, and every fresh trial, under the loving eye of Jesus, and sanctified by the indwelling Spirit, is like a fresh gale wafting us nearer and nearer to our port; to the place He has gone to prepare for us. All these things work together for our prosperity of soul. We will never think, when we get heaven, that we had one trial too many. We shall see that we could not have done without one of them, for all were so many needful lessons to instruct us in a journey through a wilderness full of temptation. Infinite wisdom has chosen them for us. I know your trials are often great, but the loving eye of Jesus is upon you, and your name is deeply engraved upon His heart. Whom He loves He loves unto death.

The eye, the all searching eye of God is upon us every moment!

It is Satan robed as "an angel of light," not Satan appearing as a fiend of darkness, that we have most to dread.

I fear we have too little contact with Christ Himself. We do not sufficiently make him our personal friend; walking with him, talking with him, confiding in him as we would with the dearest personal friend of our hearts. And yet this is our high and precious privilege. "This is my Friend," should be the language of every believer, as he points to, and leans upon, Christ.

O there is no school like God's school; for "who teaches like Him?" And God's highest school is the school of trial. All his true scholars have graduated from this school. "Who are these who are clothed in white? Where do they come from? These are the ones coming out of the great tribulation. They washed their robes in the blood of the Lamb and made them white." Rev. 7:13-14. Ask each spiritually, deeply taught Christian where he attained his knowledge; and he will point you to God's great university; the school of trial.

The Lord has laid His heavy hand upon you. All is in love. May He open your eyes to see it. He loves us too well to afflict us with out a 'needs be'. When we get above, we shall see how needful the chastening of Him who loves us, for our preparation for the full enjoyment of that place He has gone to prepare for us. Oh, what a change! from earth to heaven! From a suffering bed to a mansion of glory! You are the sufferer; but dry your tears, for home will come at last, and may we receive from His own loving lips a "Well done, good and faithful servant; enter into the joy of your Lord." I feel for you, and pray you may be sustained and comforted by God. Jesus is very near. He is ordering all things for you. He does not willingly afflict us. It is to wean us from a dying world and from ourselves. We too much grovel here. The Lord sees the encroachment of earthly ties, which leave but half for Him. Let us, then, gird up the loins of our mind, and make a fresh start for heaven. A crown of glory awaits us! Jesus, the very same Jesus, is on the throne, as full of love, compassion, and sympathy as when a man of sorrows here upon earth. Oh, the glory that awaits the Christian! By all these painful dispensations He is preparing us for the full enjoyment of that glory; glory begun here; glory increasing through out eternity. This world is not worth a thought; and we should ever bear in mind it is but a passage to a better world. Let this fresh trial, like a stormy gale, drive you nearer and still nearer to Jesus. Make Him your all in all.

We must all pass through much tribulation before we enter the kingdom He has gone to prepare for us. Let us, then, take up the cross, and follow hard after Him. A little while, and we shall be there. Sweet thought! Oh, let us try and realize it. Heaven is not so far off as we imagine. But as I draw nearer and nearer, heaven seems to open with increasing attraction; and the prospect of seeing Jesus, that same Jesus that bore all my sins on the accursed tree, fills me with joy unspeakable and full of glory.

There is nothing too small to carry to Jesus. Abroad, at home, in company, or in the street, lift up your heart, and tell Him all you feel and all you desire. Aim to have constant communion with Him. Let Him not be long out of your sight. Oh! to have to do with Jesus and with Jesus only! Do not make up your mind to do anything before you ask counsel from Him. The heart is deceitful, and will lead us astray. Let us be very jealous over this inward foe, and only consult our dearest and best Friend. Oh, He is an ocean of love! Nothing but love is in His dear heart towards His precious children.

We live at too great a distance from Christ. He wants us to experience more of His sympathy, His boundless love, His nearness to, and His oneness with, us.

One of the delightful employments of heaven will be to trace back the way the Lord led us safely, in spite of ourselves, through the wilderness world. And then shall we see how needful was every cross, and trial, and pain, and dispensation, with which our precious Jesus saw fit to exercise us.

Be of good cheer, God has sent your trial. It is a messenger of love; nothing but eternal, boundless, never ending love. God is love, an ocean of love, nothing but love. His tender, loving eye is upon you, and His loving heart is towards you at this moment. See what a God and Father He is. Soon we shall all pass away, and be done with sorrow and sin forever. A thousand times have I thanked the Lord for all my trials and afflictions. I would not have been without them for worlds. They have been messengers of boundless love and mercy to me. I do trust this will be your rich experience. Your friend and sister in tribulation.

The Lord has taken His suffering child out of all her troubles, to her happy, happy home! Long had she been refining in the furnace, and preparing for that place Jesus had gone to take possession of for her. Not one pain did she suffer, or sorrow did she feel, but had in it the tenderest love of Jesus. All was needful. He was preparing her for the full enjoyment of His presence. Shall not the Judge all the earth do right? She has made her escape from a world of sin and trouble, and from a body, not only of sin and death, but of suffering, and long a clog to her soul. She has broken loose from her cage, and is with Jesus! Oh, the happiness to look upon Him; to behold Him in all His unveiled beauties; to see Him face to face! I rejoice that she is at last released! I covet her joy.

There is nothing that can take place towards a child of God but what our heavenly Father designs, in infinite love, for our spiritual advancement, and His own glory. We are to submit to His holy will, and believe that there was a 'needs be' for it. The Lord loves His children too well to lay upon them the weight of a feather, without an absolute necessity, and without some wise and loving purpose. God deals wisely and graciously with us in all His varying dispensations. If tears could be shed in heaven, we would weep that we ever mistrusted His goodness in His dealings towards us. Let us, in this world of trial, cling close to Him, and lean more upon Him as little helpless children. Keep a constant communion with Him. Tell Him all you feel, or wish, or need.

I would not have been without my sad trials for ten thousand worlds. What would I have known of the wondrous, tender, and unchanging love of Jesus, but for my deep trials?

This poor world is but a wilderness, and, like the children of Israel, we must pass through it to reach our heavenly home. Live much in holy contemplation of the glory that awaits you. This will enable you to bear the bitter trials that daily cross your path. Carry all your difficulties, small and great, at once to Jesus. His ear is open to your requests, and he will make every crooked path straight, and rough path smooth. We are on a journey, and how soon it terminates!

Oh, how awfully blind are many who call themselves Christians! Religious formalism is the bane of thousands! They say prayers, but never pray. They know nothing of the great change from nature to grace; nothing of the new birth. They have no personal, spiritual acquaintance with Christ; nothing of real conversion. Is it not melancholy to see so many, whom we love, yet living in the gall of bitterness and in the bond of iniquity, while we know that, dying in that state, they are lost forever?

We are so prone to look to 'the creature'; and then He takes our prop away, that we may lean upon Him and upon Him only. Oh, let it be our aim, our chief business, and the desire of our souls, to walk humbly and closely with God! In a little while and we pass away; and oh, how we shall wonder at ourselves that we could have allowed any one thing to divert our minds, even for a moment, from the great, the overwhelming concerns of eternity!

There is not a single truth in God's word which will be of any avail to us, but as it is wrought out in the experience of the soul, by the power of the Holy Spirit, through the varying dispensations of Divine Providence. Thus the Israelites were led through many trials and difficulties in the wilderness, to show them what was in their hearts. We are such dull scholars; and I often wonder and wonder again at the patience of a good, gracious, and unchanging God towards us. He varies His dealings, that He might teach us our nothingness, weakness, and total helplessness.

The kingdom of God does not come with observation. The world knows nothing of what is passing within the soul of the believer; the mighty work which the Spirit is carrying silently on. The hidden evil is revealed; his soul, in sorrow, flees to Jesus; the Comforter applies the blood to the accusing and disturbed conscience; the throne is erected; the King reigns supreme; the soul rejoices; all this transpires in the believer without any outward sign, and the world knows it not. And so the kingdom of God's grace in the soul works secretly and silently, and without observation.

I thank Him for the throne of grace, where I can relieve my burdened heart, and tell Him all, keeping nothing back, good or bad. Oh, is not this a mighty privilege? The God of heaven, the Creator of all worlds, stooping in love to 'simple dust'!

It is a perilous and an awful thing to be satisfied with a form of godliness, without the vital, saving power. May the Lord lead you into an 'experimental knowledge' of Jesus. No other knowledge is worth having.

How tender and gentle are the dealings of our good and gracious Father to His child! Oh, how wisely He acts in all His various dealings with His children! He gives no account of any of His matters, but acts as a sovereign on His throne.

How often does covetousness transform itself into the shape of prudence, and thereby we are likely to be deceived. Oh for stronger faith to live above the policy and precepts of this poor dying world!

Every doctrine, as well as every word of God, is only effectually profitable as it is worked out by the trying providence of God in the soul's deep experience. Head knowledge will not do. Hearing with the outward ear does but little for the soul, enables it to make no progress towards heaven, or unfolds to us the tenderness of Christ, or the real character of God. The truth as it is in Jesus is more known in one deep trial than a year of smooth sailing. Worldly prosperity is but indifferent soil for the Christian to grow in. It rather stunts the soul.

Jesus is the very same; as full of compassion, sympathy, gentle, tender love, as when He walked the streets of Jerusalem. Is there not enough in a precious Jesus to engage all our thoughts and all our hearts? Let Him be our chief joy now. Let us keep very near to Him, and let no idol come between our soul and our best, nearest, and dearest Friend. The only way which a good and gracious God has pointed out to us in the Scriptures, in which we may be enabled to go on our heavenly journey, is by looking unto Jesus, not only when we first commence, but all our journey through.

I think, if there is a verdant spot in this wilderness world, it is where a poor believing sinner, with a contrite, broken heart, sits at the feet of Jesus. The sinner confessing, Jesus pardoning; the blood applied, and the conscience cleansed; all guilt removed, and the redeemed of the Lord rising from his knees, rejoicing in the Lord his God. Such have I often experienced, and therefore I commend it to all who are followers of the Lamb.

How many have passed into the eternal world fatally deceived by the error of baptismal regeneration! Baptized in infancy, they, were taught to view themselves as spiritually regenerated, as made the children of God; and they died, it is to be feared, with no more light and no more grace, believing they were safe. Terrible delusion!

Eternity and an immortal soul, surely, are solemn realities, and not to be sported with.

God is training us for our happy inheritance. Oh, let us try and live to it. What are the various sorrows of the way, compare with the glory that shall be revealed in us?

Jesus is everything to us! Without Him we are wretched, and with Him we have all that can be desired.

Heaven seems very near to me. It seems but a step and I am there, where there is no more sin, nor death, and where all tears are forever wiped away. This poor world is a valley of tears. I have been a child of sorrow, and yet not one trial too many have I had.

Aim to bring up your children for eternity.

Go to Jesus for all you need. Take Him as your true, your best, your only Friend. There is not another like Him. Take Him as your brother born for adversity. The oftener you go to Him, the more welcome you will be, and the better acquainted. Do not first go to an arm of flesh, and then to Christ. But go to Christ first, before you make up your mind as to the course you should take.

This poor dying, disappointing world, at best is but a cheat, promising much, but performing little! Oh, what a world is this! What a mercy that we have a Friend who rules over all, and who has said, "I am the Lord, and I do not change."

I have often thought of the goodness, kindness, and tender sympathy of God, that though man had sinned and was at enmity with his Creator, Benefactor, and Friend, so that the ground was cursed for his sake; there should yet be so much in this world to comfort, to alleviate, and delight; so much still lingering of its pristine beauty to regale and please. And if this world is still so attractive, so lovely to the eye and pleasing to the senses; what must that world be which infinite love has gone to prepare for the redeemed and pure spirits designed to inhabit it!

I need to learn to live day by day, trusting God for the daily supplies of His grace, and for the leadings of His providence; leaving the morrow in His own blessed hand, who knows how to give and when to withhold.

Walk in the fear of God, and you need fear nothing else.

Never undertake a cause without kneeling down and asking the Lord for wisdom and grace. If Solomon felt it needful to do this, well may you. Christ says, "Without Me you can do nothing."

Did you but more know the depth of that love that is in the heart of Jesus you would never be reluctant to go to Him for all you needed.

PART 3:

Every new trial, and every fresh cross, drives me into the very bosom of Jesus; and it seems as if I could lie there, and feel the very throbbings of His loving heart. I am His, and in His own loving hands, and can fully trust Him for all. In the cup of trial we are called to drink, there is no wrath, all is love; though faith may be tried, and we may for a season weep. Whatever draws or drives us to Christ is a mighty blessing. How needful are these high winds and storms to cause us to cling to our heavenly Pilot, and to speed our way to our blessed harbor of eternal rest.

The Lord's table is a season of melting love. The heart is softened; Christ crucified for my sins is placed before the eye; deep repentance and holy affection fill the soul.

This world, and all that you have loved, are insufficient to impart one grain of real happiness. You may find in Jesus all, and more than tongue can express, of what your soul needs; an everflowing, overflowing fountain of indescribable happiness and holy enjoyment.

How graciously God is dealing with my soul. I cannot describe, for language fails me, His exceeding gentleness, and His tender love to my soul. I go to Him often in perplexity, not knowing where to look; and as a babe is hushed to quietness, soothed and comforted on its mother's bosom, so the Lord calms and quiets me.

Never, never could it enter into the heart of man to conceive the rich gifts there are in the heart of Christ for His saints!

Heaven would be no heaven to me if I did not see Jesus, my best, my dearest, my constant Friend, who with unceasing patience, tenderness, and mercy, has followed me through all my wanderings in this wilderness world; and has never, no, never, left nor forsaken me for one single moment. To know Him aright is a little heaven begun below.

Oh, heaven is worth living for! A life of trial and of tribulation is as nothing when compared with the mighty blessings that await the believer in Jesus, when he drops the body of sin and of death. I have been, and still am, looking to the things that are not seen, and that are eternal.

Precious Bible! Precious revelation of God's most gracious doings of eternal mercy to such sinners as we are!

Heaven seems always before me, and in imagination I am constantly there. I long to be gone. I much enjoy, in anticipation, the blessedness of that place where Jesus is, where He unveils His beauteous face, and we shall behold Him without a cloud between. My sweetest meditation, lying down and rising up, or waking in the night, is Heaven. Oh, to enjoy unutterable bliss of perfect freedom from sin, in the presence of Jesus, my dearest, my best Friend.

"The Lord raises those who are bowed down." Psalm 146:8. How little do we think of whose care we are under, and whose loving eye is ever guiding our way through the wilderness, causing all things we meet with, to work together for our good! Thus has He led me. He has brought me into the wilderness to teach me; to lead me to cling closer to Himself; to brighten every grace of the Spirit; to wean me from a dying world; and to show me this is not my rest, because it is polluted. Here He gave me precious faith, and then tried the faith He gave. When bowed down, He lifted me up. He shut me out of the vain things of a poor empty world, and shut me into Himself.

Growth in grace is to know more of Christ, His excellence, preciousness, and fullness, through the teaching of the Holy Spirit. Growth in grace is to know more of our wretched, lost condition, our helplessness and unworthiness.

Surely the wise virgins are slumbering! Oh that the church would awaken and rejoice at the glorious prospect that is before her! The Lord Jesus is on His way!

When you enlisted under the banner of King Jesus, you commenced the life of a soldier, and are therefore called, as a good soldier of Jesus Christ, to fight manfully. Your enemies are the world, Satan, and the flesh; this last is the greatest of all; it lies down and rises up with you, and wherever you are, this enemy is always at hand.

A corpse floats down with the stream; but where there is living faith in the soul, it stems the tide, buffets with the wave, and makes its way through all that opposes it. Be of good courage, keep close to Jesus, and you have nothing to fear from within or without.

This world is nothing more than a wretched, dying vanity! But the bright world to which we are traveling has substantial blessing and unutterable happiness to bestow. Oh, then, what folly to grieve here, and allow our affections to wander from God!

Oh, for more weanedness from the world! Oh, to love Jesus more, and to have Him more in our thoughts! How soon we may behold Him in all His glory, coming in the clouds of heaven, with all His saints and holy angels!

Time is short! You have much to do for God in a little space. Eternity will be quite long enough to rest.

Oh that you may trace His dear hand in all His tender, gentle dealings. Walk doubly close to Him in the day of prosperity, and watch over your heart with a jealous eye, lest it prove a temptation and a snare.

Christianity ennobles, sanctifies, and immortalizes all the endeared relationships of life.

Ought I not to grow in grace, and in the knowledge of God my Savior? But oh, how slowly I advance to what I ought! One thing I do know: I feel increasingly my own vileness, and see increasing beauty in the gospel, and its suitableness to the needs of a poor sinner. God shows me more of my own sinful self, and more of that perfect righteousness in Christ Jesus, which is unto all and upon all those who believe.

Oh, to call the Creator, the Upholder of all worlds, mine; yes, mine, for I am His, and He is mine, and that through all eternity; is a privilege so sweet that angels might envy!

This world, with the dearest earthly creatures, could not satisfy my soul.

How delightful to live to please Him, and Him only, who died for you!

Watch against the treacherous foe we carry within!

I would be holy, even as He is holy. I am wearied with sin; my soul loathes it, and I abhor myself in dust and in ashes. Truly, I would not live always thus. Heaven would be greatly to be desired, were it only to be done with sin forever. But oh! the presence of Jesus in all His glories, unveiled to our wondering eye, will make our happiness complete. "O earth, earth! let my heart's best affections go, and trouble me no more. I want this heart only for Christ! It is His by the purchase of His blood; it is His by the conquest of His grace; and I covet it all for Him. Oh! May every throb beat with love, gratitude, and adoration to Him who has saved my soul, and redeemed me from the power of the enemy! Amen, and amen."

I look back, and sigh, and grieve, and think how many evils I could have avoided.

I feel more and more the exceeding sinfulness of sin, and my own weakness and inability to stand one moment, without the all upholding arm of Jehovah Jesus!

The way to God is so delightful, so exactly suited to a poor lost sinner; so suited to me. A way sprinkled with atoning blood; justice and mercy as a wall of defense on either side; and this way leading to such a rich treasure house, filled with all blessing for time and for eternity. All is in Jesus the way to God, the way of holiness, the way to glory.

I have to recount the goodness and unfailing mercy of my good and gracious God, who has brought me thus far on my weary pilgrimage. I have to lament my unfaithfulness and backslidings of heart from Him.

Let us often look back upon all the way our God has led us, and trace His gracious dealings at every step; and we shall not only acknowledge that He is good, but we shall aim more and more to do everything that is right and pleasing in His sight. Oh for more grace, more uprightness of heart, and more singleness of eye! It is with God we have to do, and not with man.

Keep your eye upon the cross of Christ, and you need not fear to see yourself as you are.

I have felt today much blessedness in viewing the Lord as my own and only Friend on earth and in heaven; and making a renewed surrender of my whole heart to Him, desiring above all earthly good that it should be molded according to His will, and made conformable to His likeness. There is a store of incalculable riches in Christ! He is everything to me! I could not live without Him! I could not die without Him! Heaven would be no heaven to me if my Beloved were not there!

Every place where Jesus is, and which He blesses with His presence, is sweet. He can transform a dungeon into a palace, and His presence can turn darkness into light.

Who can tell the glory that surrounds the saints on their entrance into that abode of bliss? How strange that we do not more often long to be there, freed from a body of sin and death, and a life of pain and suffering! Oh that I may be helped to keep my garments unspotted by the world; and to be ready when the summons comes!

Oh, if we did but fully believe that God will condemn the impenitent sinner to eternal perdition, we would act very differently!

If the religion of Christ is not the main business of our whole life, it is nothing, and we are nothing, and shall be found as nothing, or worse than nothing, when He comes to judge the world.

Unbelief, unbelief, oh, this is our great crime before God! We will not take Him at His word, fully believing all that He has promised. If we really believe that sinners will be cast into hell, would we not be more earnest both with them and with God? Oh yes, we would!

When I have a glimpse of God as He is in Himself, as well as what He is to my soul, I sink in all my nothingness, melted into love, at His feet. What would I do but for Jesus? "Precious Jesus! I do love You. You are the chief among ten thousand. I am wearied with 'the creature', for disappointment is written upon the dearest object here below. But in You there is no disappointment, You blessed, dearest One! Oh that I could love You as I wish to do, and serve You with all the powers of my mind and body! Let not my heart wander from You! Keep me under the shadow of Your wing until the storm of life be past."

I cannot trace a single thing I ever did in my whole life that affords me any real pleasure to look back upon.

With what a delusion Satan continually aims to blind the minds of men as to the brevity and uncertainty of human life. How often does he prevail, even with the real Christian! On looking back upon the past sixty years of my life, and forward to the little point that remains, what a dream! How like a vision does it appear! Oh, how little of it, if any at all, has been spent to the real glory of Him who gave it.

None but God Himself could bear with such sinners as we are.

I seldom rise from my knees without weeping; my whole heart melted with contrition in view of the wonderful love of God to one so poor and vile as I. Oh, how near does He sometimes draw me to Himself! And when I look around, and see so many mercies, so many blessings, such tender care in providing for all my needs, no good thing withheld; although my base heart has distrusted Him in the very mist of countless proofs of His love; I abhor myself in dust and in ashes. God has forgiven, and does forgive me, but I cannot forgive myself.

God's ear is ever open to the cry of His children!

I have never wept so much for sin as I have done lately. Often have I put up the prayer, 'Search me, O God'. The Lord has heard and answered it; and oh, if it had not been that the fountain was still open, I would have sunk into unutterable despair. He has ploughed up the fallow ground afresh of my poor heart, and the view presented has prostrated me in the dust. If ever I felt what a broken heart and a contrite spirit was, I have of late. Oh, the evil that is there covered over by the rank weeds of 'self love', self complacency, or self in some hideous form or other, that is not discernible until the Holy Spirit makes it known. He is pleased to show us enough to make us cling closer to the cross, to make Jesus more precious, and sin more hateful. But while I have thus been led of late to mourn so much for sin, I have never felt pardon so abundantly manifested. Oh, keep close to the cross!

I see myself more and more, every hour, a poor sinner, unworthy of the least crumb that falls from the Master's table. But I see, at the same time, Jesus a great Savior, divinely able, and most lovingly willing, to save the chief of sinners, even me. No one can tell how this thought fills my heart with contrition, and my eyes with tears.

Oh that we might always endeavor in all things, in thought, word, and deed, to please God; setting aside everything which is not connected with His glory, and contemplating all things and all events more in the light of eternity!

How jealous ought we to be over our hearts. When we find a traitor there, how earnest should we be to bring him directly to the Savior, that He might enable us to place our foot upon his neck, while He himself subdues the evil that He hates.

Had God not tried me in the furnace of affliction my loss would have been immense. I thank Him for my deep, deep cup of sorrow. Whatever draws or drives us to Christ is a blessing. We then breathe a holy, heavenly atmosphere, and see the poverty of all other things to make us happy here or hereafter.

We shall soon meet where we shall be all of one mind, in a brighter, happier world, surrounding the throne of Him we love. Blessed be God for this prospect! It often causes the dark cloud to withdraw, and the weary soul to take fresh courage, and press onward, and look upward. Blessed is the hope of the Christian!

Oh, what a mercy to have a throne of grace, and a tender, compassionate, loving Christ to go to at all times, and under all circumstances! A genuine welcome; no frown to fear; no distant look. Oh that we all might live upon

Him, moment by moment! For this reason He takes away our props, that we might lean fully upon Himself.

Did you but see your children standing on the edge of an awful precipice, and know that none but God could prevent their destruction, would you not cry day and night to Him? What can be compared to the eternal death that awaits them, if they die unconverted? Will you not pray, that your dear children may escape from the wrath to come? In proportion as you feel the infinite value of their immortal souls, you shall feel anxious for their salvation.

Our heavenly Father knows better how to control and direct our concerns than we know ourselves. Oh, to be among the number who wholly trust in the Lord!

Nothing but the power of the Holy Spirit can convert the soul. The Word, and the preaching of the Word, pass for nothing, unless accompanied by the Holy Spirit. If God has begun His work in the soul, God will complete it, and all sin cannot destroy it. Salvation from first to last is of God. God begins it, God carries it on, and God will finish it forever. Blessed be His holy name!

May the little trials we have may be so sanctified, as to draw us near to Christ, and make Him more precious than ever!

I weep that I am such a sinner, while I stand in wonder and astonishment that God can love and does love, such a one as I, and having loved me in time, will love me through eternity.

Our happiness does not depend upon a favorable change of circumstances or of place, but upon a submission of our wills to the will of God; a complete surrender of every desire and wish to Him who is acquainted with what is best for us.

What a chamber of iniquity is the heart, all hidden and unknown, until God in mercy shows it to us, as we are able to bear the disclosure!

Let us not be faint and weary because of the hardness of the way. It is the Lord's way. Thorny and steep though may be the ascent, when we reach the summit we shall be well repaid for all our labor.

Great things often spring out of little things. Let me entreat you to look to Him continually, for counsel to direct in little as well as in great matters. Oh that we might both be led to sit more constantly at the feet of Jesus, looking up, like little children, into His face to catch His smile and watch His eye; to see what He would have us to do, seeking nowhere else for comfort and guidance but in Him!

Be very cautious to whom you open your heart. Make no one your confidant but Jesus. Oh, commune with Him of all that is in your heart. If you are wounded, go and tell Christ. If you are in need, go and tell Christ; the silver and the gold are His. If you are in trouble, go and tell Christ; and He will deliver you out of it, and you shall glorify Him. Live upon Him as little children would live upon a dear, kind, and tender father. Oh, how happily will you then pass on your way! If at any time you are in perplexity or difficulty, through your own imprudence or otherwise, do not go to an arm of flesh, nor sit down to consider how you are to obtain deliverance; but go directly to Jesus, and tell Him all, all; and He will appear for you, and bring you out of all.

I have been thinking of the worldling's happiness; it never satisfies; it affords no real enjoyment; it does not reach the soul. Ten thousand worlds could not satisfy me, now that I have tasted the unspeakably precious love of Christ!

It is not change of place or circumstances, but Christ alone, that can make us truly happy here and hereafter. God would have us cease from these things, and live upon Him alone for our enjoyments!

I often think how mysterious are the ways of God. It is our mercy, however, to know at all times that He is directing our steps, and that not a circumstance in our lives but is included in the everlasting covenant that is ordered in all things and sure. It is a great thing to be helped to be satisfied with God's dealings and ways, and not to dictate to Him, even in our minds, what we conceive would be better for us.

Remember, the more your sermons are filled with Christ, from first to last, the more will Christ honor your ministry. There is no preaching like it. Never be afraid of not finding something new to say of Him. The Holy Spirit will supply you with matter as you go on. Never doubt it, never fear. The whole Bible points to Christ, and you must make it all bear upon the subject. Christ is the sum and substance of the whole!

I never knew a man who seemed to find his way to one's heart as Mr. Evans does in his preaching. He arrests your attention, instructs your mind, and captivates your heart. Oh, what a precious gospel we hear; doctrinal, practical, and experimental religion beautifully blended!

How deep are the riches of the love of Christ!

Oh, what a God do you serve! How infinitely condescending in all His steps towards you, and how deeply indebted are you to give yourself entirely to Him!

What should we do were it not for a throne of grace to go to? In all my troubles and difficulties I flee to Christ, for none can help me but Him. You do the same. You need not carry your own burdens, when Christ has commanded you to cast them on Him. Learn in the early stages of your Christian pilgrimage to go constantly to Jesus. Live upon Him for all you need for both soul and body, for He has redeemed and will take care of both.

Oh, how precious is Jesus to a poor seeking sinner! What a mercy that when we sin we have in Him an Advocate, and a fountain still open to wash away our sin, and always welcome to come; never so welcome to Christ as when we feel our misery and poverty, our nothingness and unworthiness. He it is who gives the broken and contrite heart that He delights to look upon. The enemy would sincerely keep us from Christ when we feel our vileness; but it was for sinners Jesus died.

Oh, it is sweet to live a life of holy dependence upon the Savior! I find it more and more so every day. May He save you from trusting your own heart, or leaning to your own understanding in anything.

Let us think a little of our home, our pleasant home. A precious Jesus waiting to welcome His weary pilgrims there. A sweet home indeed! Our Father's home! And a happy meeting with all who are dear to us and to Christ. No more separation; no more sickness, no more sin, nor more labor, but one endless scene of love and happiness!

How often has an unkind look or word proved a blessing to my soul! It has made me flee to Christ; and there I have found no unkindness. He has appeared, at such times, more than enough to make up for the lack of all 'creature love' and created good.

How wretchedly poor are my best conceptions of this most glorious work of salvation! Dear Lord, enlighten my understanding, that I may more and more see the infinite value of this wondrous work of everlasting love; and may my base ingratitude and unbelief never be thorns to wound You afresh.

What a mercy, of more value than a thousand worlds, to walk in the fear of the Lord all the day long; to be enabled to live above the smiles or frowns of this world, and to find the love of Christ all satisfying to our souls; to feel all 'creature love' swallowed up in Christ, and to know that He loves us better than we love ourselves.

As soon as I take my eye from Jesus, and look for anything like comfort from this world, or look within for something to rest upon, I begin to be in trouble, and have again to run into the name of the Lord, which is a strong tower to my soul at all times! Oh, why look to 'creature love' when the love of Christ is always the same?

Still traveling on, I humbly trust, through this waste howling wilderness, to my heavenly home. I need to look more to Jesus, that I may be strengthened for this continual warfare, for so it is with me. But am too often looking to some broken cistern still; but afterwards can say, when enabled to turn and take a fresh view of Christ, I do prefer Him, with all my trials and cares, to all that the world calls good.

By constantly poring over anticipated troubles, we lose the sweet enjoyment of present mercies in the expectation of future evil. I pray to be enabled to praise Him for the present, and trust His love for all that is to come.

There is an inexpressible sweetness in the thought, that salvation is not of works; and that our full and complete acceptance is not in our wretched selves. It is all, all of grace.

Oh, the hidden evil of the heart, unknown and unfelt, until the Spirit of Christ sees fit to reveal the depths of iniquity that are there. It is a sickening view; and were it not that Christ Jesus came into the world to save sinners, I would lie down in utter despair. Nothing but the precious blood of Christ can wash my guilt away.

O Lord, help me more and more to cease from man, whose breath is in his nostrils, and to expect nothing but evil from an evil world!

It is good to walk by faith; to feel dependent for all, and to come to Him as little children for all we need.

Oh, the sad levity and trifling of some, even of the ministers of Christ! I am aware of the same evil in myself, and by these things lay up material for bitter repentance.

Oh how lovely, how good, exceedingly good, is Jesus Christ to unworthy me! He is enough to satisfy my soul.

When disappointed in the creature, and I turn with a sickening feeling from the world to Christ, I find here no disappointment. Here is fullness of joy, an ocean of love, a heart to feel and sympathize, an eye to pity, and a power, an infinite power to supply all my needs, to comfort my drooping spirits, to refresh my fainting heart, and lift me with joy and peace in believing. Jesus is an all satisfying portion, and He is my portion, O my soul.

Some new lesson in the school of Christ is daily, no, hourly, to be learned; some hidden evil to be felt; some new enemy to be encountered; some fresh, precious views of Jesus to be obtained.

I increasingly feel that this poor world is not my rest; it is polluted! Go where he may, rest where he will, trials and crosses await the Christian.

When trials press upon my mind I must arise and carry them to Jesus. To whom else can I go? I would not often tell the dearest friend in the world what passes in my mind; but I can disclose it all to Jesus! I can and do unbosom myself to Him whose compassions fail not, and who remembers I am but dust; yet pities and loves me better than I love myself!

I never fail to find that trials drive me closer to Christ, and quicken me in the exercise of prayer.

The essence of real religion is intimacy with God.

Remember that God has to do with the heart. 'To this man will I look, even to him that is poor and of a contrite spirit.' Humility is one of the sweetest graces of God's Spirit. Earnestly seek to know as much of your own hearts as will keep you sitting at the foot of the cross; and at the same time to know as much of Christ's heart as will enable you to rejoice in the fullness and sufficiency there is in Him.

My beloved children, never, never omit secret prayer! Remember, the first departures from Christ begin at the closet, or rather in the heart; and then private prayer is either hurried over, becomes a mere form, or is entirely neglected.

A few more years, and we shall be done with all things here below, and eternity, with all its glorious realities, will burst upon your view! Oh, then, live for eternity! Think much of your blessed inheritance there, and let the glory of God be dearer to you than your own lives.

Beloved, in all your many difficulties and trials, do not first go to an arm of flesh, nor sit and ponder what you shall do. But go directly to your dear Savior, and ask earnestly for wisdom and grace to guide you through them. Watch the leadings and openings of His gracious providence, and follow on as He leads the way, and He will make even these things to work for your good. Cast your cares, as they arise, upon Him who cares for you!

Avoid trifling, lukewarm professors. They are the bane of the church of Christ! If you can do them no good, they will do you much harm.

Beloved, go to Jesus for all you need. Lean upon Him. There is a fullness in Christ, treasured up for you, that the highest angel in heaven cannot fathom! Tell Him all that is in your heart. Lay your case before Him as if He did not already know it. This is the sweet simplicity of faith that

Christ loves. You cannot come too often. Bring to Him your little cares as well as your great ones. If anything is a trouble to you, however small it may be, you are warranted, no, commanded, to take it to Him, and thereby you glorify His name.

Oh what a mercy is a throne of grace! Wherever you are, at home or by the wayside, lift up your heart to that precious Savior who has manifested so much love to your souls.

Oh, it is good to look back and trace His dealings and His wondrous works to us! Taking thus a review of these gracious things, under the teaching of the Eternal Spirit, so far from being puffed up, they will lay us low in the dust under a sense of our base ingratitude towards Him, and the wretched returns we have made for such distinguishing mercies.

Nothing tests or strengthens faith so much as the trying dispensations of God toward His people. The furnace destroys everything but the pure gold! Nothing but real faith can endure the heat of the fiery crucible, and, what is strange, it grows in the fire!

In Christ, I discover such a fullness, such a sufficiency, such goodness, and boundless, matchless love, that at times I can but kneel and weep! My mind is led from earthly things to longing desires after conformity to His holy likeness. Oh, to be holy! How beautiful does holiness appear to me! To be holy is to be happy. May the Lord sanctify us! A little while and we shall be done with those things that but too often encumber us, and then, Oh what glory awaits the believing soul!

I feel my vileness, my unprofitableness, my woeful shortcomings, and am thankful if I can but only creep to the foot of the Cross, and there repose my weary soul, refreshed by one look at Jesus, who died for my sins. But oh, I want to be more conformable to His lovely image, to be sanctified, body, soul, and spirit, and to have every power of my mind under the constant influence of the Holy Spirit.

Mysterious are the ways of God! This bereaving providence has done more to wean me from the world, and show me the importance of eternal things, than you can imagine. Blessed be God for all His dispensations, the evil as well as the good. My severe trials have awakened a general sympathy among the dear people of God, who have visited and endeavored to comfort me. But vain is the help of man. God alone can comfort. I see love and mercy directing this stroke, and I trust it will be abundantly sanctified to my soul. I know it is for my good that I have been afflicted.

Tribulation must be felt, or it would not be tribulation; and it is needful. I think I have learned more of my dreadfully wicked heart, and the preciousness of Jesus, during this trial, than I ever learned before. It has been a bitter discipline, but I hope, with God's blessing, it will bring forth the peaceable fruits of righteousness; tending to wean me from the world and from self, and causing me to know where my great strength lies. I failed not to thank my God, and to implore His aid to strengthen me, and enable me to bear up under this and every other disappointment and trial, through what His infinite wisdom should see fit I should pass while on my pilgrimage through this wilderness.

I feel my poverty and my need of Christ more and more. My choicest seat is at the foot of the Cross! When I can but view His bleeding wounds, and obtain one glance by faith of His gracious countenance, it is worth a thousand worlds to me. Nothing else can give me joy and comfort. I find it is the safest to keep close to Jesus; and as I came at first, so I come again and again. In this way the foe is defeated, and my soul is melted with love, while He lifts upon me His heavenly countenance.

I rather decline much communication with worldly people; for if one can do them no good, they are sure to do you some harm.

Oh, the sweets of true religion! To know the Lord Jesus is our Friend surpasses every earthly good, and is better than the possession of a thousand worlds. To have Him to go to; to lay before Him all our needs, to express our fears, to plead His promises, and to expect that because He has promised He will fulfill; is worth more than all the world can give. His ear is ever open to the prayer of His people, and, though hell and death obstruct the way, the weakest saint shall win the day.

I am strong, and in good spirits! for my Friend above reigns, and He has enabled me to cast every weight of care upon Him.

May the Lord fill your hearts with peace and joy in believing, and lift you above this poor, fleeting, perishing world.

Oh, how far, how very far do I fall short of what a true Christian ought to be! I grieve and lament my shortcomings, and long to manifest myself, by practice as well as by profession, a lowly follower of Jesus Christ.

All we have to do in this valley of tears is to press forward to the glorious prize He has placed in our view, looking continually to Jesus, trusting not to our own strength, but waiting in humble dependence upon Him for all our sufficiency to carry us on, and to enable us to hold out unto the end. This world is not our home; we look for a better. His people are pilgrims here on earth, and generally are a poor and afflicted people. They have not their portion here as thousands have; their portion is to come. Their names are written in the book of life, and were written before the foundation of the world. They are as dear to Him as the apple of His eye. Then what have we to fear? nothing; but everything to hope.

Blessed be God, who sent His only Son to pay our debt, to rescue us from the power of Satan, to cleanse us from all our guilt, to clothe our souls with His righteousness, and thereby give us a rightful claim to a crown of glory.

Beware of the form of godliness without its vital, its blessed power!

Remember that you have not to do with man but with God, and that God has to do with you. He scrutinizes the motive, searches the hidden spring, regards the principle, and by Him actions are weighed.

Live and think and act with eternity fully in view!

There is not a circumstance in my whole past life, but what I have reason to mourn and weep over in the dust before God. It has been evil, and that continually. Never, never publish my worthless life. I am ashamed of it, and abhor myself in dust and ashes. God knows I do. I see nothing but sin in myself from the moment I knew anything to the present instant. Lost as I was, vile and polluted, Jesus made the atonement required, paid my debt, bore the penalty, washed me in His precious blood, and the Holy Spirit in due time unveiled my blind eyes to see my lost condition, wretchedness, and misery; and then led me to the fountain opened for sin and uncleanness. There He cleansed, clothed, and saved me! But what returns have I made for all this rich display of mercy? I must put my hand upon my mouth, and my mouth in the dust before Him.

How few follow hard after their glorious Leader, the Captain of our salvation! There are few who seem to be in right down earnest in this holy, heavenly warfare.

There is a divine reality in the religion of the Bible, but it must be experienced in the soul to learn its mighty value and infinite blessedness. I meet with but few who have this divine echo in the heart; the soul's experience harmonizing with the revealed word of truth.

Why do you stand outside when there is room in the heart of Christ for His every needy child?

Oh, this precious Jesus! how can we love Him enough? We shall love Him as we desire to, when this poor body of flesh is thrown off and we see Him as He is.

How many ways the Lord takes to teach His children, and to wean them from the creature and from themselves!

God does nothing in vain towards His own people. He loves us too dearly to afflict us arbitrarily or for nothing.

We are so prone to look to the creature, and thus God removes our created prop that we may lean more simply and entirely upon Him, and upon Him only. He is teaching some hard yet precious and, perhaps, needed lessons; but the issue will be your deeper holiness and His loftier praise and richer glory.

Cast your present burden upon Him from whom comes all help. Is He not a very present help in every time of trouble? Why should you carry a heavy burden, when Jesus has undertaken and is better able to bear it for you, and stands ready to transfer it from you to Himself? "Cast your burden upon the Lord, and He shall sustain you."

Everything around us, viewed in relation to eternity, is alarming! The unconverted are passing into the world of woe, the Church is slumbering, error is prevailing, worldliness abounding, and the love of many for the Lord and His truth is waxing cold.

Do we really believe that there is a hell and that there is a heaven?

Temptation is a test, tribulation is a discipline, and trial is a school. All are essential to our perfect education for eternity.

Try and realize the nearness of heaven to you. It will enable you to walk more above the world, and incline your heart to seek a closer acquaintance with God as your reconciled Father in Christ Jesus.

Dear friend, make God your Confidant. Carry to Him all your needs, disclose to Him all your sorrows, confide to Him all your secrets, confess to Him all your sins. He will do all, soothe all, supply all, and pardon all, for who is a God like Him? He cares for you, His loving heart is towards you, His unslumbering eye is upon you. Oh, how condescendingly kind and gentle is Jesus to poor sinners who feel their need of Him, and are conscious that they can do nothing without Him! You will always meet with a welcome from Jesus, come when you may, and how you will.

Prayer, precious prayer, how can we live without it? What could I do had I not God to go to? Oh, it is my chief joy and comfort to throw open every avenue and chamber of my heart, and disclose to Him all.

Oh the comfort, that while crossing this sandy desert we are privileged to hold converse with Jesus, telling Him as our dearest Friend, all we need and all we desire.

Oh, what would we do in a world of sin and sorrow without Jesus! Heaven itself would be no heaven were He not its attraction, its glory, and its joy. His name is Love, and an ocean of love is His heart.

Is it not strange that we cling to this shadowy, fleeting life as we do?

Jesus came to my help, raised my eyes to Himself, drew me closer to His heart, hushed my mourning, and enabled me to repose my sorrow upon His bosom.

Oh, for stronger faith and more filial submission to all His blessed, loving, holy will!

May the presence of the Lord be with you, may His love comfort you, and may His arms encircle you, to preserve you from all evil!

Who can portray the joy of the soul the moment it is freed from the flesh, and finds itself in the immediate presence of God, encircled by all the holy angels, and the goodly company of glorified saints, who stand round about the throne?

May we be enabled to follow on to know the Lord more fully, and be more engaged in the contemplation of heavenly realities, so that we might live more above the poor things of a dying world. This poor world is not our rest; and God will not have His people rest in anything short of Himself.

It is our loss, when we permit ourselves to be so absorbed with present passing trifles as to lose sight, even for a moment, of the glories and attractions of that upper world into which we shall to a certainty soon enter. I think I could sometimes sit all day long looking up into heaven; heaven seems so opened to my view, so near, so real, so blessed and holy. I seem to stand upon its verge, and beneath its very portal.

It is through Satan's devices that God's Word is cast aside, and human wisdom and tradition is set up in the place of God's revealed truth.

In a little while we all must stand at the bar of God. Short and uncertain is our time here. Eternity, with solemn realities, is before us. God has, in His rich mercy, left us a divine direction to show us plainly the way we should take, turning neither to the right hand nor to the left. The path is there prescribed to those who desire to do God's holy will and to walk in the same.

Alone with God. Sweet moments these, to a saint of God; rich the privilege to be closeted with Jesus. To get closer to Him, to hear His voice, the gentle whisper of His unchanging love, to be enabled to unbosom our whole hearts to Him, confiding to Him all their secrets. Is not this a mighty privilege?

How mysterious are often our Father's dealings with us; and yet all is infinite love. Not a cross, not a pain, not a trial but is given in the tenderest love to our souls, dear to Him as His own beloved Son.

Do you not love to think of heaven? Not only as a place of rest- rest from all care, and conflict, and toil- but above all, a perfect rest from sin. But more even than this, as the place where we shall see and be with Jesus, and be perfectly like Him. To behold the once despised Man of sorrow, seated upon His throne, encircled by the host of heaven, will be a glorious spectacle. And shall you and I be there? Shall we not together shout our song of praise to Him who bled for us, died for us, who paid our mighty debt, and who so patiently bore our ingratitude and coldness, our wanderings and lack of love, throughout our wilderness journey? How unwearied has been His changeless love towards us.

One precious view of Jesus will more than repay us for all our sufferings and afflictions and crosses here, were they ten thousand times more than they have been. To look upon that countenance which so often illumined with its smile our dreary path, filling our souls with joy unspeakable and full of glory, and which, when our hearts were so broken for sin, because it was sin against One who so loved us, and whom we loved, that we were ashamed to look up and knew not what to say, even then has He beamed upon us His look of forgiveness- oh, will not this be heaven! Long we not, dear friend, to see Him, that we might thank Him again and again for all His mighty love and great goodness, marvelous loving-kindness towards us poor sinners, eternally lost but for Him? There are seasons when language quite fails me to express what I feel towards Him, and then how do I long to depart that I might tell Him all I cannot tell Him now.

God is in small events! How unspeakably precious and sweet it is when we can believe that God our Father in heaven is absolutely directing the most minute circumstance of our short sojourn in this wilderness world! That nothing, however trivial, takes place, whether it relates to the body or the soul, but is under His control; in fact, is ordered by Himself! But how hard to believe this, particularly when things look dark, and we cannot discern the way we should take. It is, then, the province of faith to wait upon the Lord, keeping a steadfast eye upon Him only; looking for light, help, and deliverance, not from the creature, but from Jehovah Himself. Well may it be called precious faith! How happy do those travel on, whose faith can discern God's hand in everything. But I fear the number is very small who so live. I cannot imagine how those who deny God's particular providence can get comfortably on, for they must perpetually be confronted with minute events in their history as mysterious and baffling to them as greater ones.

It is a consolation to know that Jesus reigns, and that all things, all creatures, and all events are in His hands and beneath His control.

PART 5:

How is it that the Lord places His people so frequently, and keeps them so long, in the furnace? When one trial is over another comes, scarcely, sometimes, allowing breathing time between! Wave resounding to wave! Oh, it is because He loves us, and will have us know it. And when trouble comes, small or great, we then shelter beneath His wings, or nestle within His bosom, and feel the very throbbings of His heart. Who can sound the depth or measure the dimensions of the love of God towards His people- its depth, its height? Eternity alone can unfold it. It passes knowledge. Oh, it is sweet to repose in His bosom, and shelter there until the storm be past.

It is only by constantly looking to Christ that we can get joy and comfort. Thus, looking to Jesus and going to Jesus, we travel through this intricate wilderness comfortably and safely to our home in heaven.

May we be led daily, hourly, to look more simply to Jesus; leaning upon Him for all we need for body and soul, for time and eternity. I find that the more I am enabled to live upon Him, the happier I am; and it is the only comfortable way of getting through a host of trials and difficulties, and of renouncing the world, the flesh, and the devil. May God give us all more of the sweet simplicity of faith.

The more we feel the exceeding sinfulness of sin, and are led into a just view of our own most wretched helplessness, the more we shall value the great and all-glorious atonement made for sin; and in proportion also will Jesus be precious to our souls.

Oh, what a privilege for such worms of the earth to have fellowship with the great and mighty God of the universe, and such nearness of access to the very heart of a precious Jesus!

What poor creatures we are, and what a wonder a holy God should love us so!

How is it that we are not always rejoicing? Because of our unbelief! What a conflict have I had lately with that monster!

Our friends who sleep in Jesus only cross the threshold a little before us, and if we are real followers of Christ, we shall soon meet them, and that to part no more. Your heavenly Father has taken one that was dear to you, because he was dearer to Himself, and He wished to have him in the full enjoyment of Himself a little sooner than you would be willing to part with him. Blessed are the dead that die in Jesus!

All we have to do is to keep a steadfast eye upon Christ, and live upon Him moment by moment, coming to Him for all our supplies; as children feeling their dependence on a parent's love, come to a loving father, nothing doubting His power and willingness to grant them all that they need.

This light affliction is but to draw you off from the creature and closer to Himself. He would empty us of self that He might fill us with His Spirit, and thus be more closely assimilated to His image, more like Jesus. You are blessed of the Lord; dear to Him as the apple of His eye. Jesus is our Sanctifier, and He is fitting us for His beatific presence in a brighter, happier, holier world, where there will be no more sickness, nor sorrow, nor sin. Then shall we behold Him in all His glory, and be forever with the Lord.

As I have lain on my sick bed, I have been favored with much of His most precious presence, and can scarcely call any circumstance a trial when the oil and the wine has been so richly poured into my soul. How unspeakably precious is our Jesus. How good and full of love in all His dispensations with His people. I truly feel that goodness and mercy have followed me all the days of my pilgrimage, and will continue to follow me to its close. He has engaged to bring us safely through all, making us more than conquerors over all. "Call upon me in the day of trouble, and I will deliver you." This exceeding great and precious promise has been to me like untold gold. I have sometimes thought, surely I shall weary Him out by my continual coming; but not so. The oftener I come, the more welcome. I feel I can cast myself into the very ocean of His love, in which the feeblest saint may safely swim.

Men think lightly of sin; not only sinners, but the saints do not view it in its proper light. Sin is not a light thing in the sight of God. The Church of God is asleep. Christians have too light views of sin.

We need more of the descent of the Holy Spirit in His almighty power, that sinners may be converted and saints thoroughly awakened. Oh, when shall the Holy Spirit be poured upon us from on high? Oh that in infinite love He may condescend to bow the heavens and come down!

Christ is my physician. I love to open my whole heart to Him. I would have no concealments from His blessed eyes, sinful as I feel myself to be.

Jesus can manifest His wondrous love to the vilest and most unworthy of His creatures. Jesus is very, very precious, and full of tender compassion.

The world, with all its riches and honors and glories, is dross compared with the wealth and blessedness that is yours in virtue of your oneness with the Lord Jesus.

Cultivate this heavenly communion, this holy, sanctifying familiarity with the Son of God. Allow nothing to come between you and your best Friend.

Oh, how uncertain are all events in this changing world! We are here for a little while, and then pass away; the believer to his happy, happy home in heaven, prepared for him by infinite and eternal love. How is it that we strive so hard to build our nest here, and cling so fondly and with such tenacity to the creature? Did we fully believe all that Christ says to us, how much more willing should we be to depart and be with Him!

What would I, what could I do without a God to go to? Oh what a transcendent blessing is a throne of grace in a time of trouble! What a bosom is God's where we can pour all our sorrows, and disclose all our needs, assured that He not only hears us always, but can do for us better than we can possibly conceive of, for all power is His. I believe that our severest trials will, in the end, throw off their somber disguise, and stand before us as among our loveliest and most precious blessings. "Find rest, O my soul, in God alone; my hope comes from Him."

I sympathize much with your loneliness, and wish you were nearer to us. But Jesus is always at hand, ready to comfort when all other comfort is gone. This may be a time when He deigns to draw you closer to Himself, to show you more of His loving heart, and to teach you how much you need Him at all times. Endeavor to get closer to Him as that Friend, and Husband too, that sticks closer than a brother.

How is it with your faith? Are you keeping a steadfast eye upon Christ, who has promised to supply all your needs? Or, are you looking more to an arm of flesh? If you are, God will disappoint you. When you have a need, look first and go first to Jesus, and let Him not take the second place in your estimation. Go in the simplicity of a little child, pouring all you need into His willing ear and tender heart.

There is no school, in the believer's training for heaven, like the school of affliction, in which to attain to a knowledge of the character of God.

We are not to be like the world around us, but are to see God in everything, and in every act; and walk humbly and closely with Him.

We need in our present exile to dwell more on heaven than we do; to sit more in heavenly places; to be looking away from present trials, afflictions, and disappointments to the things that are unseen, and eternal. How much better would we then bear our present woes; the roughness and the privation of the homeward pilgrimage. Oh, dear friend, when we reach that world of glory and of bliss, and see Jesus as He is, we shall marvel and wonder, and were it possible, should weep, at the thought that we could have been satisfied to remain so long the tenant of this body of sin and of death, and not pant more for the disembodied, unrobed spirit, and so be instantly and forever with our best Beloved.

What a marvelous spectacle is this! a poor sinner and a holy Lord God meeting together at the blood sprinkled mercy seat! Is not this most blessed? I often go burdened, and come away light as a feather, nestling beneath the very wing of the Savior, and listening to His well known, "Fear not!" I disclose to Him all that is in my heart, and He unveils His loving, tender, forgiving heart to me.

Dear friend, keep close to Him. Let not the world and its cares come between you and Christ. If a cloud intervenes, rest not until it is withdrawn. Go, and go again, and should a shade still obscure the glorious vision, return not from His presence until even its shadow has dissolved into full, unclouded light.

How precious does Jesus appear to my soul. I lie at His feet as the lame beggar at the beautiful gate of the temple, asking an alms; helpless, yet waiting; believing and hoping to receive a smile from the beamings of His countenance.

Who can subdue our inbred sins but Jesus? As well might we attempt to upheave a mountain, as to argue with and remove even a solitary corruption of our fallen nature. But if we carry it at once to Christ, He will do it all for us! This is one of the most difficult, though needed, lessons in the school of Christ. I seem myself to be only just beginning to learn it, and therefore am brought often to take the lowest class, and come as a little child to Jesus to do all for me, and all in me. My own imagined strength has all vanished, and my boasted wisdom turned into foolishness.

O eternity! With all your solemn realities, how is it that creatures of a day think so little of you! A few more stages and you and I, dear friend, will be there! How soon, how very soon, we shall be fitted for the companionship of Jesus Himself, and shall be with Him, beholding Him in all His unveiled loveliness, and bathing in the ocean of His love! Does not the thought often gladden your heart, while it dissolves in sweet contrition, that ever it should have sinned against One who so loved us as to lay down His precious life for us?

What a costly proof has He given you of His love in laying down His life for your soul's salvation!

Infinite wisdom and infinite love cannot mistake. Trials, losses, crosses; all, all are needful, and when we get home we shall plainly see how wisely they have been all ordered. Let us, then, leave our concerns in the best possible hands. He will do all things well for us, and in us, and by us. We are His and He is ours. What need we fear?

Christian love and sympathy are very sweet, and we should ever be grateful for them, for the creature is just what the Lord makes it to us. But, oh, the delight of having that Friend of friends to whom you cannot only open your heart, but who can bear your trouble for you, feel for you, help you, comfort you, and that effectually. Such is Jesus, our true and best friend.

Satan will keep us poring over our difficulties until they grow into mountains in our imagination. We have but a very imperfect idea of Satan's power and malice towards us. Our only help is to flee at once to our Stronghold, our Refuge, our Hiding place, where alone we are safe. Oh, how safe! We may hear the lion roar, but he cannot reach us. Sheltered beneath the wing of Jesus we can defy his malice and his power.

What a confidential, holy communion might be kept up between us and our best Friend now in heaven, and our souls on earth. He is in heaven for us, waiting to be gracious, listening with the deepest solicitude and ardent love to all our requests. Make all your requests known unto Him, with thanksgiving.

Our God so orders all things connected with our eventful journey as either to allure or drive us to Himself. Is it not humiliating that we so constantly require such sharp discipline to bring us to know more of His boundless, matchless love? He bears us continually on His heart, and in all that concerns us He is equally concerned.

Oh to be more like Christ! This should be our whole aim; to be conformed to His image, and so show forth His praise. How few bearing the name of Jesus know what it is to deny themselves for His sake; and are conformed to His likeness. Let us aim to be here as Christ was, and to be satisfied with the way He deals with us in all things.

My joy is always more or less mixed with tears; joy and sorrow. It is a pure mixture, and God would have it so. Joy in the Holy Spirit, and sorrow for sin.

Oh what a God He is to all who know and trust Him! How safely may we, at all times, confide our all in His blessed hands. Who is like our God? What heart so full of love as His?

The prospect of soon being with Jesus is to me a most delightful thought.

Only think for one moment how inexpressibly dear you must be to the heart of God!

In every position in which God may place His children, He designs some good towards them; and it ought to be our prayer, honest and fervent, that He would, by His Spirit, show us why He deals with us, and the profit He would graciously have us reap. God acts intelligently, wisely, and righteously in all His dealings with His saints. Nothing is done without forethought and plan. Nothing is done without an object and a design. There is NO CHANCE with Him. All, all is part and parcel of a preconceived, arranged, and defined scheme. Let us, then, quietly repose in Him; and seek first His glory in all things, leaving Him to care for, and dispose of, all secondary considerations.

It is good to have our thoughts continually heavenward; to be looking to the things that are not seen, and are eternal. This will help us to sit loose to the things which are seen and temporal. A few years, short and fleeting, and we pass away from hence. Then, of what little importance is everything here which is not closely connected with our present advancement in the divine life. We are only pilgrims, seeking a city that is to come. We shall soon be admitted into the glorious presence of Jesus Christ! Let this blessed prospect nerve us to do and to endure the will of the Lord in all things; and to see that we grow in grace and in the knowledge of Jesus, that our wandering, deceitful hearts might be kept in close converse with Him in all that we have to do.

I long, ardently long, to depart and be with Him; to see Jesus; to enjoy Him with fullness of joy; to be like Him, perfected in holiness.

A Father's ear and a Father's heart are both open to our faintest breathings. Only go as a little child with all your requests, and He will answer. Oh, what a Lord we have to do with- mercy, mercy, unbounded mercy!

Oh that the Lord would but open the eyes of poor lost sinners, and show them the inefficiency of everything else but the knowledge of Christ Jesus to make them happy here and hereafter!

Oh, how awful to go blindfolded into that lake that burns with fire and brimstone!

Nothing but the constraining love of Christ will fully constrain us to holiness.

It is a pleasant thing to me, sometimes, to anticipate the eternal rest that awaits me, my happy home, the home provided, and the welcome from so many that will greet my arrival within its gate of pearl. But first of all, and best of all, to see Jesus, my dearest, my only Friend, whom I love, and desire to love, above all earthly beings. Oh to behold Him! to know Him! to recognize that benevolent and transcendent countenance that so often beamed upon me, unworthy as I was, in the weary days of my pilgrimage!

When we can bring all our poor concerns, little and great, and our poor hearts, too, to Him, and lay them all before Him, I am persuaded we need fear nothing, for God will order all things for us, will bless us, make His love known to us more and more. And we shall see His dear hand held out to help and guide us through this wilderness safely and honorably, to that happy home His love has prepared for us above. Oh to love Jesus, and to know that He loves us! To aim, although we constantly come short, to glorify Him in all we do and say, and to let that be our highest aim.

Let us aim to live more above the world, and look alone to the Bible as our divine directory in all things, and alone to our God for His approbation. Let us be ashamed of nothing but sinning against Him, and grieving His Holy Spirit. Oh, if we did but this at all times, how much more would we adorn the doctrine of God our Savior in all things, and how much easier would we pass through a world lying in wickedness!

What poor creatures we are when old age, with its thousand infirmities, comes upon us, reminding us that this is not our rest, and that we must be preparing for the rest above. Happy day, happy hour, when that takes place!

What subdues, what breaks the heart like communion with the Holy Lord God, unfolding and revealing Himself in Jesus?

May you be helped to live decidedly for eternity, with your eye upon that glorious crown which Christ has promised to those who overcome! But a short time you have to glorify Him; aim to do it in all things and at all times. Live to God, live for God, and God will take care that you have all you need while you live. He will give you grace and glory, and no good thing will He withhold if you walk uprightly.

Deem no sin a trifle. Beware of the first enticement to sin! You will have need of much prayer night and day, that God may guide and uphold you, preserving you from every snare that the wicked one might throw in your way; and that, sensible of your weakness, you might rely more upon His almighty strength to carry you safely through all the temptations that lie in your path. The devil will tempt; the world will tempt; your own carnal nature will tempt. And all your own strength of resistance is perfect weakness. How can you stand against this threefold troop, but as your Savior puts strength in you? Seek this in earnest prayer, and, with Christ strengthening you, you can do all things.

I sometimes think it is a greater trial to be rich than to be poor. Of this I am quite sure, that riches to the Christian are a great snare, as well as a great trouble, and entails more anxiety and sorrow than real pleasure and enjoyment.

I feel a blessed nearness to heaven, to Jesus. My soul holds converse with Him. Sweet it is to lie as a helpless babe at His feet; passive in His hands, knowing and desiring and doing no will but His. What a mercy to have one loving bosom to flee to! One truly loving heart to confide in, open to the faintest breathings of the troubled soul, the fullest utterances of the sorrowing heart! "Precious Jesus! How blessedly dear and near to me are You at this moment! Keep sensibly close to me. Lift up upon me the light of Your heavenly countenance, for it is better and sweeter to me than life."

What a mercy to have such a One to lean upon, who can and does enter into all our little needs and cares! By this constant living upon and traveling to Jesus we become more conformed to His lovely likeness. I would encourage all I love in the Lord, to keep up this holy fellowship and intercommunion with their dearest and best Friend. Let Jesus be all and in all to us. Let us feel that we cannot live without Him.

My afflicted friend, nothing is too hard for God to
do; nothing impossible for Him in whose arm we trust. He
hears your every sigh, and His tenderest sympathies are
towards you. Rest in His unchanging love, and be assured
His unslumbering eye is ever over you for good. Confide in
Him at all times, under the darkest clouds. This is the time
to exercise faith in the living, loving God. All our trials are
tokens of a Father's love, and sent as trials of His
faithfulness, and as increasing our knowledge of, and
acquaintance with, Himself. As a loving father pities his
children, so He pities us.

We all have a talent committed to our trust; let us
be prayerful to know what it is, and diligent to lay it out for
God.

Religious formalism is one of the most extensive
and fatal snares of souls. There is in most a constant 'saying
of prayers', without praying; a perpetual repetition, without
feeling. The heart untouched, unmoved, unbroken. How
few who profess to be converted understand anything of the
new birth! They have heard of Christ, but do not
experimentally and personally know Him. They have never
repaired to Him with a broken and a contrite heart. But to
be brought as a poor sinner to His feet, there to lie until He
speaks pardon and peace to the weary, heavy laden soul, is
quite another thing.

Marvelous are the dealings of God with us! Let us
trust and praise Him here, and hereafter we shall fully
know why we were put in the furnace, and confess that love
kindled, and love watched, and love brought us through it.

Dear friend, before long we shall lay aside this frail
and suffering flesh, and wing our way upwards to join the

heavenly company and be with Christ. We shall see Him face to face who loved us, and who with love drew us to Himself. What shall we, what can we, render to Him for all His great, distinguishing goodness to us?

It is no small matter to be a consistent Christian.

I am more and more convinced that it is neither riches nor honor nor power that can make a man happy either in this world or in that which is to come. Nothing on earth or in heaven can do this but a knowledge of JESUS. How vain are all things beneath the sun!

Oh, who would not live and strive for heaven! Perfect holiness! perfect happiness! No sin, nor sorrow, nor cruel death, can ever enter there!

I find it sweet to retire and be alone with my best Friend. What a privilege to open our whole heart, and lean, like John, upon the Savior's tender, sympathizing bosom! What on earth is like this? A broken heart, a helpless and powerless soul resting upon the arm and the heart of Infinite and Eternal love!

All His dispensations, however trying, are in love to our souls. He wishes us to cling closer to Himself, and would remove everything that comes between Him and His child. He desires, too, that we shall bear more of His own image, and be more weaned from a passing world and dying creatures.

The promise, "Call upon Me in the day of trouble," has been to me more than untold gold! I never knew Him to fail. If He did not remove the trouble in my way, He did it in a far better way. Recollect that His ear is open to our cry, and He loves to hear our pleadings.

The sweetest and safest life is to lean upon Him as a little helpless child, even as a child weaned of its mother, quiet, submissive, clinging.

If you feel your love to Him chilled, go and tell Him, and He will warm it with His own precious and unchanged love. Go just as you are; let your state of mind and body be what it may, you will always find a welcome from Jesus.

Let us try to live more decidedly for eternity, lessening our hold of the trifles of this poor world, and anticipating the kingdom, the crown, the glory, the welcome that awaits us.

The wicked are only the Lord's rod to drive us nearer to Himself, that we might know more of His pity, power, and love.

There is no chance with God. Every circumstance connected with you was ordered before your had existence. Each event, small and great, each step you take, was predetermined and provided for. God knows all, and does all, and will do all things for you. I would have you rest on this truth, that in the everlasting covenant of grace, all our history was shaped and anticipated; so that in the full belief of this truth, the mind, under all present dark and inexplicable circumstances and events, is at once at ease. Oh, could we but look into God's heart, His dear, loving heart, and see how precious we are to Him, how truly He is watching over us, wisely directing all the incidents and circumstances of our history for our good and His own glory, how soon would all our present grievances vanish, and we sit as little, weaned children at the feet of Jesus!

Oh, when we think how short time is, how uncertain is life, and that a vast eternity awaits us; how unwise we are to allow ourselves to be entangled with earth and earthly things!

How awful it is to see God's creatures living as if there were no eternity before them!

My dear friend, we are on our way to a land the inhabitants of which shall not complain of sickness or suffering. Death cannot enter there. And while still here in this poor world, we have a God to go to, who will never leave nor forsake us, but bring us where we shall forever be done with sin and sorrow. Now, this blessed hope revives often our drooping spirit. The Lord knows we need this cordial on our journey through this poor, trying wilderness, and supplies our needs, small and great. He is concerned in all that concerns us. We must go forward, growing more acquainted with ourselves, as poor and needy; and with Christ, who is our storehouse, full of grace and truth, to whom we have but to go and tell Him, and His heart is open to us in a moment.

Life here without Christ is misery indeed! But oh, to know Him, to love Him, to be borne in His tender bosom through this wilderness of sin and sorrow, is a happiness indeed which cannot be described, and can only be known by experience!

Pray for your enemy. He is only an instrument in the Lord's hands to accomplish His own loving purposes towards you. God is in all things.

"Do not be afraid." The Lord reigns! "Do not be afraid." He is the same gracious God, yesterday, today, and forever. "Do not be afraid." All things are working together for your good. You and Christ are one, and your interests cannot be divided from Him. You are His, and He is yours. Keep close to Him, and carry to Him all your concerns, and He will do all things well for you.

Oh, what a companion is Jesus to a poor helpless sinner while journeying through a wilderness filled with all manner of evil and beasts of prey! We shall soon see Him. Then let us keep our garments unspotted from the world, walking in holy, filial obedience to His divine commands.

What an unchanging Friend is Christ to us! For though He chastens, yet it is all in love, that we might know Him better, and give to Him our heart's chief affections. Oh, He is altogether lovely! The chief among ten thousand! Love Him, and manifest your love to Him, and He will come and manifest Himself to you!

To lift up Christ is the way to draw poor sinners, and to lift poor saints above their darkness, doubts, and misgivings. To see the rich fullness there is in Jesus for the poorest, the vilest, the most helpless that ever called upon His dear name, oh, this is gospel. Did He ever refuse one who came to Him? No, never; and He never will!

There is nothing worth living for but Jesus; to serve, honor, and glorify Him, enjoying His presence here as a pledge of its enjoyment throughout eternity. Is it not a solemn thought? I cannot tell you of His love. Language fails me to express it. He is love, all love, nothing but love.

The Lord has indeed abounded in mercy towards me, upholding in many of life's troubles, comforting, encouraging, and guiding when there was no eye to pity and no hand to help but His own. I have ever found Him a very present help in time of trouble. I can truly say it has been good for me that I have been afflicted.

"Why me? Why me? Lord, why is it that You have had thoughts of mercy towards such a one as me? From everlasting to everlasting You have loved me. Why me? Why me?" Oh, what a difference grace has made!

As the believer advances in the divine life, he sees less and less to boast of, and more and more to humble him. There are none so proud as those who are ignorant of themselves and of Christ. Their imagined righteousness keeps them back from the Savior. They come not as lost and undone sinners, but fantasize they see some little good in themselves.

A mere profession may carry one in such a way as will please the flesh; but as Christ walked through the wilderness, so must His followers more or less take up the same cross.

What is this fair world? I feel such a weariness of this world that nothing here gives me anything more than a momentary, passing pleasure, and it is gone at a glance. Oh for heaven! Nothing else will satisfy my longing soul but the sight of Him it loves. Jesus is all in all to me, and He will be all in all through eternity. Praise the Lord, O my soul; all my inmost being, praise His holy name!

Religious formalism is the fatal ruin of thousands of souls. I refer to the mere religious professor, the unconverted formalist, those who have not passed from death unto life. They have heard of the Savior with the outward ear; have gone to church, have said many prayers, and have done many things, and yet have only a name to live while they are dead. How many, I fear, deceive themselves in this respect! I tremble for such! Let us make our calling and election sure, not by looking to ourselves, but by looking to Jesus.

God directs all our affairs; and although we so little think of Him, His thoughts are ever towards us for good, in His rich mercy overruling our mistakes for our good and for His glory.

Dear friend, let your sad heart rest upon the loving heart of your Savior. Keep close to Christ. Holy, constant communion with Him is the life of religion in the soul.

Dear friend, let us live more in sweet fellowship with Jesus, and when we pray in secret; no ear hearing and no eye seeing us but His; let us never be satisfied without sensible communion with Him. Jesus is the one Friend, and the only one, to whom you can unveil your whole heart. Is He not precious to your soul? Is there one like Him on earth or in heaven? "Precious Lord! to behold You here, to have but a glimpse of Your lovely countenance beaming upon us in love, is a little heaven below. Then what must it be when we shall see You face to face in all Your unveiled beauties above!"

A few more fleeting years, and you are gone forever! And where are you going? What is your fate and condition in the eternal world? A dying bed is no place to prepare for eternity. Oh that you were wise, and would consider your latter end, and apply your heart unto wisdom!

May God open your eyes to see your need of a Savior, and lead you to the feet of Jesus, the sinner's Friend.

We have a dear, compassionate Savior to deal with, who knows all our weaknesses and infirmities, and will give us what we need if we only repair to Him in the simplicity of little children. Oh, how ready He is to listen to all our requests!

If we really believed that every unconverted person we meet with, dying so, would be lost forever, would we not be in earnest to warn that soul to flee from the wrath to come? Would we not avail ourselves of every favorable opportunity of praying for them, expostulating with them, and beseeching them to consider their latter end and turn to the Lord that they might be saved? I know there is much wisdom to be exercised to know how and when to speak, all of which the Lord will give to those who are earnest in asking for it. Eternity, with all its solemnities, is before us! May the Lord make us faithful.

There is a fullness in Jesus that can supply the needs of the millions who repair to Him, and yet He remains as full as ever.

If we desire to know more of ourselves as we are in the sight of a holy God, it is not by contemplating our sinfulness, but by looking to Jesus. A close and constant view of His perfect holiness, His expiatory sufferings on the Cross, His ignominious death, His unparalleled love; will show us the evil of sin, and of ourselves as sinners, as nothing else can. Then it is we see sin in its true light, and lie in the dust at His feet. One clear believing view of Jesus exhibiting His loving, sin-forgiving, compassionate heart;

breaks our heart, and dissolves it in penitence and love, under the sense of sin fully pardoned.

Let us aim to act, and speak, and walk as if Christ were at our side! And so He is, though we may not be sensible of it.

One reason why we go on our way halting and wavering is, that we do not realize the truth of what awaits us above. Deal more closely with this, and trials and disappointments will less affect you. It is by keeping up a constant, believing communion with Jesus that will secure this blessing to us. What is our present life? It is but a vapor, and soon passes away. But what is our life to come? A state of holy, happy being, as long as the existence of God. Then, cheer up! Go to Jesus, and tell Him all that is in your heart. He will bow the heavens and listen to all you have to say to Him.

Have you surrendered to Him your whole heart? Then blessed are you. Fear not; He will watch over you day and night, for He cares for you. Do not attempt to transfer your concerns from His hands into your own. He knows the end from the beginning; and infinite wisdom, power, and love are all engaged on your behalf. If you have committed your soul, of more value than ten thousand worlds, to Him, cannot you trust Him to regulate and conduct your earthly concerns? A fretting against God's providence is very dishonoring to Him, and causes Him to leave His perverse child to have, for the time, his own way; and then how bitter it is in the end! The Spirit is grieved, the sensible presence of Christ is withdrawn, and the soul is left in trouble and sorrow and darkness. It is a mercy under such circumstances that our God changes not, or we would be consumed. Live upon Him as a loving Father; the Father of the fatherless, and of the motherless too. He will be to you both, and that Friend that sticks closer than a brother. Lean upon Him, and He will support you under all the trials of life, for He is a present help in every time of trouble. I, for one, have tried Him, and He has never failed me in any one instance. Give yourself up wholly to Him, body, soul, and spirit. Go and tell Him all. You need not shrink from opening your whole heart to Him. He will keep all your secrets, and will do all things well. He will withhold no good thing. What He does withhold He sees would not be for our good. Learn early in life to trust Him with your all, and He will be all to you.

If we could grieve in heaven, it would be in the recollection of our unbelief on earth. Help us, blessed Lord, to trust in You under all circumstances, and more than ever when thick clouds gather around us, and we walk in darkness and have no light!

Jesus is an ocean of love to my soul, while I increasingly feel that I am the poorest of the poor, and feeblest of all His flock.

You must feel your lost and undone condition before you will ever come and cast yourself at the feet of Jesus. The same blessed Spirit who is showing you the vileness of your own heart, will in due time show you also the heart of Christ. Only look into His loving heart, and yours will rejoice with unspeakable joy. Do not look at your own heart, but at the heart of Christ.

If He does not answer at once, it is because He loves to hear the pleadings of His child. See in how many instances Christ appeared not to hear, when at the very time He designed to grant the petition.

The riches and honors of this poor dying world cannot compensate for the loss of the sweet, precious, and life giving influence of the Holy Spirit within.

There is never one petition put up by a child of God, however faint, but He does hear it. One little mite of faith will send it not only into the ear of God, but into the heart of God too.

Only let us live upon Jesus practically and habitually, and we shall lack no good thing.

Every dispensation of His providence has a voice, if we did but listen to it, and come before our loving Father and inquire of Him. God can make even a sick room a Bethel to your soul! All places where He is, is a little heaven below! His presence sweetens every bitter cup, and makes afflictions light.

PART 5:

Oh, the comfort, the inexpressible comfort of a throne of grace! It is the only verdant, refreshing spot in this world's wide wilderness. To have the sensible presence of God, the heart of a loving Father to confide in, who is able to do all and more than we require; to have Him always near, His hand ever stretched out; Oh, the comfort! This is my sweetest spot and chief comfort in earth's wild wilderness, where I carry all my cares and troubles, and am ever sure to receive a welcome in the face of a reconciled Father. Oh, the loving heart of Christ! Although He knows our ten thousand infirmities, He does not turn a deaf ear to our poor supplications, but with His own blood blots out all their imperfections.

Why does God discipline His own children but to teach them their own weakness and helplessness, and to make them cling all the closer to Himself. All our trials and afflictions are to wean us from the creature, the world, and self; to find all we need or can wish in the fulness of Jesus. "From among all the families on the earth, I chose you alone. That is why I must punish you for all your sins." Our chastisement is one proof of God's love for us.

Oh, what poor creatures are we, and how needful to have One all mighty and all love to keep us in the way, in spite of our wretched proneness to wander far from our best Friend! How often, had He left us to our own way, we would have ruined ourselves, soul and body, have made shipwreck of our faith, and have been lost forever! Oh, the patience of this good and gracious God, who bears with our woeful manners in the wilderness from moment to moment, and deals not with us according to the least of our sins!

Beloved, you belong to Him who loves you, and who in infinite wisdom and wondrous love will take His own way, His wise way, His loving way, which will be the best for you through time and eternity.

What wretched work it is to depend upon the creature, who changes and varies in all its feelings, purposes, and affections every moment! But our best, dearest, and only Friend changes not. He cannot change, because He is God. A God, too, all sufficient and all mighty. Such is your Friend and mine. So never be cast down. If He has given His Son for us, will He withhold any other good thing? He knows the end from the beginning. We know nothing beyond the present moment. If left to ourselves, we would destroy ourselves; but He has promised to provide, and to care for, and to preserve us, even to the end.

I feel much sympathy for you in this afflictive visitation of our God. It has a voice. He does nothing in vain. He does not afflict willingly. It is, among other designs, to wean us from the world and from ourselves, and from those creature ties which so much draw our hearts from Him, so that we have but half for God. Let us gird up the loins of our mind, and start afresh for heaven. Why does He afflict and correct those whom He loves? It is to cause them to live more above a dying world, walking more humbly and closely with Him. He is jealous of our love.

Never sit down and reason what you should do in this or that perplexity, but go at once to the Lord with it, distrusting your own heart; which is deceitful above all things; but trusting Him, which you may safely do. We are poor blind creatures, and need this Heavenly gracious Guide.

How tenderly is He watching over us! His sleepless eye of love ever upon us; a Friend to guide us through the wilderness, encircled, as we are, by a host of beasts of prey. How wondrous that we are not lost, and lost forever, living in a world lying in the wicked one! No power short of Omnipotence could preserve us from his malice, or foil his deep laid schemes for our ruin. What a debt of love we owe Him who, seeing our danger, ran to our rescue, and undertook our eternal salvation!

A needy sinner and an all sufficient Savior can walk sweetly together.

I wish only to live to show my love to Him, and to manifest the power of His grace in one who in herself is one lump of sin and defilement. How marvellous that the Lord should select out of the mass of the world's sinful beings such a one as myself to show forth the power of His redeeming love and grace! Every fresh manifestation of this love breaks the heart, and humbles the soul even to the dust!

Time is hastening us on, and the moment will quickly come when our dearest Friend will claim us as His own and for Himself. Then we shall see Him face to face; and who will shout the loudest in glory? I think I shall. For, what has He not forgiven me? No tongue can tell how my heart goes out, at times, in wondering gratitude and adoring love towards Him. Such is the Lord Jesus that angels themselves know not half His worth. It is sinners, poor sinners like myself; helpless, lost, ruined in themselves; who alone can appreciate the glorious finished work of

Jesus. My soul at this moment; weeping while I write; rejoices with joy unspeakable and full of glory in God my Savior.

Let us live as candidates for a crown of glory. This will keep us above the trials and the trifles of time.

When we turn from earth and gaze upon the glorious prospect that is before us; when we see what rich provision is made in the gospel for such poor sinners as we are; when we see Jesus at the right hand of God waiting to receive us home; when we realize that a very few steps we have to take and then we will be done with time, and a vast eternity burst upon us with all its solemn and glorious realities, oh, how does the world, with all its tinsel and toys, its emptiness and nothingness, sink into the dust beneath our feet! The present world is but weariness, disappointment, and vexation of spirit. Take it in whatever form you may, it brings its troubles and its sorrows.

What debtors we are to grace for opening our eyes to see our need of Jesus, and our hearts to receive Him as the best and dearest of God's blessings to this fallen world!

Nothing is too trifling to bring to Him, which is a trouble to us. It is better to go to God than to the best, the wisest, or kindest earthly friend. Only let us come with the one request which presses the most upon our hearts, to our Guide, our Protector, our Provider, our best Friend and Brother.

How are you traveling heavenward? Are you enjoying the light of His countenance, without which nothing on earth can give true happiness, either here or hereafter? Is Jesus precious? Are you enabled to say, "My best Beloved is mine, and I am His?"

Child of God, Jesus loves you and is watching over your every step through the wilderness. And although you are prone to forget Him, He never for a moment forgets you.

Alas! we live so below our high and heavenly calling, our glorious and eternal destiny!

The day my beloved pastor died, I could have danced for joy, I so vividly and sensibly realized the scene which was taking place between Jesus and himself. I could imagine I heard the "Well done, good and faithful servant, enter into the joy of your Lord!"

"And God shall wipe away all tears from their eyes; and there shall be no more death, neither sorrow, nor crying, neither shall there be any more pain: for the former things are passed away." Rev. 21:4 Do you not almost envy those who have escaped from sin and sorrow and suffering, and are so signally honored as to see Jesus, to bask in the full sunshine of His glory, and to sit forever at His feet? See the loved ones enter the gates of heaven; angels their attendants! See the glorified, loving Savior holding out the golden scepter, and saying, "Come, you blessed of my Father!" Could we be so selfish as to wish them back? Oh no! No more pain, no more sighing, no more sorrow, no more sin!

The humble, penitential, minute confession of sin will keep the conscience tender, create a watchful spirit within, sanctify the heart, and draw us closer and closer to the Cross, and to the Christ of the Cross. Thus go to Jesus.

He is with you in all your concerns, in all your trials, in all your blessings, in all your sorrows and in all your joys. His dear eye is ever upon you for good. He loved you with an everlasting love, and with loving kindness drew you to Himself. Veil no secrets from Him. Keep an open heart with Christ. If your love is cold, He will warm it. If your spirit is depressed, He will raise it. If your corruptions are strong, He will subdue them. The oftener you come the more welcome you will be. You cannot weary nor wear Him out!

Time is short, and eternity with all its solemnities will soon burst upon our view! And yet how many who profess and call themselves Christians fritter away their little measure of time in the baubles of this present evil world! Is not this the worst species of madness? May the Lord make us faithful to Him, urging all we love to flee from the wrath to come, pointing them to the Lamb of God whose blood cleanses from sin and sanctifies the heart!

How often we detect ourselves endeavoring to build our nest below, and get wounded by thorns and thistles, with prowling beasts, the voice of the roaring lion seeking for his prey! What a mercy that Jehovah is round about His people, defending them, and watching over them with a sleepless eye, in their eventful and perilous journey homeward! Let us take the world just as God makes it to us, and desire no more than what He gives. To the believer, this world is a great snare and hindrance! The flesh lusts after it, and we require to be constant in prayer to repel its assaults and to resist its seductions.

Dear friend, we are but shadows, passing from shadows, to solemn and glorious realities. We live in a dying world. Death seems stalking about, summoning many to the judgment seat of Christ. What a mercy to be found ready; and when we meet Him, to recognize in the face of the judge upon the throne, the Savior who hung upon the cross; our dearest Friend who died for us, that we might live forever! My own mind is kept sweetly staid upon God, and my eye, in a great measure, fixed upon eternity, to which I am fast approaching.

This poor world is but a wilderness. And who would desire to dwell forever in a wilderness?

Oh for hearts to feel His great goodness, in all the ways He takes with us!

Yes, we are traveling home to God. Our princely mansion is above, prepared for us from the foundation of the world by the hand of Him who loves with an eternal love. Let us be satisfied to be but strangers and pilgrims here in a strange land; looking and longing for the time when He will say to us, "Arise, My love, My fair one, and come away!" We do not know how soon our journey may terminate. Let us be ready; our lamps trimmed, and brightly burning.

I am fully persuaded that formality is the bane of spiritual religion; religion of form without power; of possession, without recognition; satisfied with the performance of a duty, without the sweet enjoyment of a privilege.

How vain it is to look for happiness in this vile and rebellious world; a world lying in the wicked one. God never designed that His people should have a resting place here, where sin and sorrow meet us at every step. In Him alone we can rest. And when faith is tried and exercised, how pleasant to feel that we have this rest; a rest in His changeless love, deeper than the ocean, vast as eternity.

How sweet is close, confidential communion with Jesus! How fully we can then unveil all our hearts to Him; disclosing every secret; making known every need; and bringing our hidden enemies, our corruptions, to Him, that He might slay them before our eyes!

God is love! Nothing but love to His beloved ones! One ocean of love! Love in all His varied dealings and dispensations of His all wise providence. Dark clouds may hover over us, but love is embosomed in them all. The atmosphere of heaven, too, is love. And before long our bark will float in that infinite sea! What a prospect lies before us!

Oh, He is a jealous God, and will have us lean, not upon the creature, but upon Himself.

These very trials, which now seem ready to crush you, are among the "all things" that are working for your best and eternal interests. The Lord your God is at this moment watching over you for good. From everlasting He has loved us, and will love us through all the varying, shifting scenes and dispensations of His loving providence.

It is sweet to traverse this wilderness with our hand in His, safely led along each narrow path we tread. None but Jesus can make us happy here or hereafter.

Look often at your eternal inheritance. Take your walks by faith in the garden of love above. See Jesus there no longer wearing the crown of thorns but the diadem of glory! Let us give to Him an undivided heart.

What distinguishing grace to us, which has opened our eyes to see our danger and our Refuge; which has led to God's well beloved Son, to be saved in Him with a present, sure, and everlasting salvation!

Let us think more of what awaits us. This will sweeten present trial, and subdue a repining and complaining spirit. We must converse less with the conflicts and trials of the way, however painful, and more with the glory that is to be revealed. Let us draw near to Him, and He will draw near to us.

The formalist and the Pharisee! There is, perhaps, nothing more difficult than to bring a poor formalist out of his religious formality; or a poor Pharisee to drop his filthy rags, and come to Jesus just as he is: blind, naked, wretched. An 'empty sinner' and a 'full Savior' can alone walk together!

Dear friend, when He raises His chastening hand, run at once into His bosom! You cannot lie long there without feeling the throbbings of His loving heart; and this will heal the sorrow, quell the fear, disarm the rebellion, and peace and rich consolation will be the blessed result.

I not only love Him for what He has done for me, but for what He is in Himself; the chief among ten thousand, the altogether lovely One!

Why should Christ care for us, vile creatures? Oh, what a Savior is ours!

Whenever any cross of whatever kind comes in my way, I take it at once to the Lord. It is, thenceforth, no more a trouble to me. He makes the rough places smooth and the crooked paths straight.

The more I read the Bible, and the closer my communion with Jesus, the more persuaded I am, that so matchless and wondrous is the efficacy of that atonement He has made to Divine Justice, the vilest sinner that breathes the faintest, believing cry to Him for mercy; even at a dying moment- He will hear and save. The thief on the cross found it so!

The broken and the contrite heart God will not despise. There are few who view sin as it really is: a rebellion against the best of beings, the holy Lord God. And many such, without any true self knowledge, take up a profession of religion, float but upon the surface, and imagine they are in reality what they are not.

The life of God in the renewed soul is an astonishing thing. How this great and mysterious work is carried on must be a study and a wonder to the angelic world, and a wonder often to the Christian himself. We do well to watch the dealings of God with us, tracing His love and power in counteracting and overruling, subduing and sanctifying, thus fitting us for the kingdom of glory. May the Lord keep us, and cause us to see that we have but one thing to do, which is, to aim in all things to glorify and honestly to walk with Him.

A constant resort to the Fountain open for sin and uncleanness keeps the conscience undefiled and the heart tender, humble, and loving.

We live in such poor, frail bodies, it is all of mercy that we do not suffer more than we do. Sin, sin has done it all, and sorrow follows close upon its steps. Every pang should remind us of this, and remind us, too, that God has something better in reserve for us who love Him.

How condescending is Christ to one unworthy of a single crumb of mercy from His hands! But so it is! He will, in the exercise of His own sovereignty, have mercy upon whom He will have mercy, and He has had mercy upon me!

We have to contend with a host of enemies, all opposed to the progress of Christ's kingdom. What are we to do? Carry them to Jesus to subdue them for us, for we have no power in ourselves. If we attempt to subdue even one small corruption in our own wisdom and strength, we fail at once, for the smallest will be more than our match. Christ has reminded us, "Without Me, you can do nothing."

We must have more to do with eternal realities. Let us relinquish the poor trifles of earth, and fix our thoughts, and affections, and hopes more on the future.

Our precious Jesus, who deserves ten thousand hearts, if we had them, receives, alas! but half a heart, while the world would retain the other half.

The morning is to me the sweetest and most important time of the day. I then enjoy much of the presence of Him whom my soul loves; and without these sweet visits from Him, what a wretched void would this world be to the Christian! Oh for closer communion, holier intimacy, with the Father and His Son Christ Jesus. This is what we need to raise us above earth, and inspire our soul to depart and to be with Christ. We too much cling to earth and its trifles, forgetting that glory awaits us, and that an instant may put us into its full possession. How much we need to be constantly reminded of this!

It is a mercy to know that the bounds of our habitation are fixed; that is, appointed by Him who cannot err, and who sees the end from the beginning.

We live in a mournful and dying world. What a poor world, if this were to be our all! But to God's children it is but the passage across the desert, in which we are schooled and prepared for the Canaan Jesus has gone to prepare for us! But how do we murmur, often, at the training we have to go through; at the hard lessons we have to learn!

What a hospital is this world! There is but one remedy for all it's evils; the precious blood of Jesus, God's dear Son.

How mysterious are the ways of God! They are often to us a great enigma. But what we don't know now, we shall fully and eternally know hereafter. By all the varying dispensations of His infinitely wise providence, we are being disciplined for the glory that shall be revealed in us.

Afflictions, trials, and cares are the medicine of the soul, bitter for the present, but most salutary and healthful in their hallowed result. How little do we know, or still less can we judge, of Jesus' love to us while passing through a dark cloud. This is the time for faith to repose sweetly on the faithfulness of our unchanging God and Father. Let us then wait, and watch, and pray, looking unto the Lord, whose love never varies. He is doing all things well. Only trust Him, and never doubt, though you cannot discern a ray of light. Place your hand in His, and He will gently and skillfully lead you through every dark providence. Beloved, what an ocean of consolation is this!

I shall not be long here. Heaven looks very attractive. No more tears, no more parting, no more sin there. Who would not live for this glorious eternity!

Oh, how faintly do we realize the wondrous blessings that await us- the fulness of joy, and the pleasures that are at God's right hand! Oh, that we would lived up to them! This passing world engrosses too much our thoughts and time, that we forget the Lord is caring for us, ordering all our concerns in such a way as that we need be anxious for nothing. And all we have to do is to rest upon Him as little helpless children would do upon the tenderest mother. A mother may forget, yet God will not forget us!

Oh what love, that He should ever have descended from His exalted habitation in glory for the express purpose of suffering in our stead, fulfilling the law, atoning for our sins, leaving not one unpardoned thought, word, or deed; then rising from the grave, proving thereby that He had conquered all our enemies, and ascending up on high as our Redeemer, taking possession of heaven for us until He shall have brought home the last elect vessel of mercy!

Do not be satisfied with a little when there is such a rich abundance treasured up in Christ Jesus for us.

Why does the Lord employ the chastening of trial? Is it not with the view to draw us closer to Himself! Is it not to weaken the world's attractions, teaching us that this is not our rest, for it is polluted?

Ten minutes at the feet of Jesus, in a full view of His love, while confessing sins and shortcomings; sins we know already pardoned; yet sorrowing that we should ever grieve One who so tenderly loves us, is a happiness I would not exchange for millions of worlds!

Oh, what a poor wretched exchange professors make when they barter the blessings of a close walk with God, for the beggarly enjoyments of an empty, disappointing world!

If we would keep under control the old nature within us (which can never be mended); and the world outside us (which will ever be what it is); it must be by the increase of every grace of the Spirit within us. Faith in Christ will overcome the cunning world outside us, and the more subtle world within us.

It is no common journey we are upon. Every step of the way is important, and fraught with the deepest interest. God the Father is watching every trembling step we take. God the Son tenderly and graciously enters into all our difficulties, discouragements, and conflicts. God the Holy Spirit instructs and leads us onward, whispering words of comfort, and imparting new life and energy to our minds, by leading us constantly to the Fountain of living waters.

It is a melancholy spectacle to see many who seemed to run well for a season, slacken in the race, and afterwards grow weary, and turn back, and walk no more with Jesus. It is to the flesh so self denying a way; and its pleasures and joys so entirely internal, apart from anything external and visible; that the mere nominal Christian, the religious formalist, soon wearies, turns back, and finds that he was not a true pilgrim.

You and I have but a little while to honor God. Eternity, with all its solemn realities, is before us. Let us not lose a moment of the little space that is left us. Every thought, every word, every step is all important. We must live for God, and for God only. To Him we belong. He has redeemed us at a vast price, and we are His and His alone. Living for Him here, is a pledge of our being with Him throughout an endless and ever increasingly glorious eternity. God be praised for such a hope beaming with immortality beyond the grave!

We were traveling the broad road to eternal woe when Jesus met us and turned our feet into the narrow road that leads to eternal life. What could move His heart towards us? It was love; love from everlasting, and love to everlasting. And it is that same love that still watches over us day by day, hour by hour, moment by moment. And although we often loath ourselves, His love never varies. Is it not surprising that He can love us while we hate ourselves? But such is our Jesus. He is ours, and we are His.

The Lord is good, but how little we understand of His goodness! But a blessed eternity will be ever unfolding it to our hearts. The marvel is, that we are so well satisfied to remain where we are, and are not longing more to depart and be where we shall behold Him as He is in all His unveiled beauty and excellence. If the 'drops' we get here are so sweet and refreshing, what must the 'ocean fulness' be!

Is it not marvellous that after all our ungrateful returns and sad departures, He should yet stand with open arms to receive and welcome us back when a fresh trouble brings us to His feet? None but Christ could or would do this!

Nothing in the Christian's life happens in this valley of tears but what God overrules for our best interests. Every event in God's loving dealings is designed to draw us sensibly nearer to Himself.

Let us apply continually to Jesus, and not fail to take our little matters as well as our greater ones. I often find that it requires stronger faith to carry minor concerns to Him than weightier ones. Our lives are made up of little things, like small links in a great chain, forming a complete whole.

We should see His loving hand in all the varying dispensations of His righteous providence. Let us aim to walk by faith in this poor world, through which we are traveling home to a better world. Our ever vigilant foe, the devil, seeks to entrap and wound us; while we have a yet greater enemy within, ever ready to listen to his subtle reasoning. How much need have we to cry to the Lord, "Hold me up, and I shall be safe!"

I can seldom feel the love of Christ without a sensibility that moves me to tears. To think He should ever set His heart upon such sinners as we are; so love us as to lay down His life for us; and still love us in spite of all our wanderings and shortcomings, coldness, barrenness, and forgetfulness of Him; to love us notwithstanding all! Is it not enough to cause us to weep, and to lay ourselves in the dust at His feet, that, in return, we love Him so little?

In all the difficulties we meet in our pilgrim way, let us not sit down and brood over them lest our heart deceive us; but go at once with them to the Lord, making Him, with an open heart, our Confidant.

Let us view the world as passing away, and we ourselves passing away with it. It matters but little whether we are rich or poor, learned or unlearned, for soon we shall be with the Lord, who will come and receive us to Himself. Let us be watchful against the world's entanglements, gathering up our garments that they trail not upon the earth.

What a mercy to know that I am in the hands of One who loves me better than any earthly being can, and better than I can love myself. I feel so sweetly to rely upon the tender care and watchful providence of God, that my heart often overflows with a sense of His goodness and my own unworthiness; and that He should condescend to look upon such a one, and above all to love so worthless a sinner as myself.

We shall have to praise and bless His holy name throughout eternity, for every trial He has been pleased to give us. God is love; and all His purposes towards us are unchanging love, eternal as His being.

May the Lord keep us humble, meekly sitting at His feet, feeling our own wretched weakness and liability to fall, and enable us to look to Him for strength, wisdom, and grace, and above all for precious faith that we might hold fast our confidence to the end!

I firmly believe that when my eyes close on earth, they will instantly open upon Jesus, the first precious object I shall see!

What a God is our God! Who would not love Him! So good, sympathizing, and full of love! Oh for a tongue to praise Him here! We shall be fully able when we reach 'home'.

Little faith can get to heaven, though strong faith will bring us greater comfort, and the vessel will hold more of the coming glory.

We do not expect to travel through this wilderness exempt from its thorns and briers; but it is well when we feel Jesus is with us, and we can lean upon His arm, and often repose our weary heads upon His loving bosom, while He speaks to us and says, "Take courage! It is I. Don't be afraid." You need have no troubles- take all to Him, who will arrange them better for you than you can for yourself. Only beware of sitting down first to consult your own heart, and then, when this is done, to think of going to Jesus for help and counsel. Go at once to Christ! Whatever happens, go and tell Jesus, making Him your Confidant, your Friend, your All.

It is sweet to feel Jesus' love kindling in our hearts, enabling us to draw sensibly near, telling Him every need, and wish, and fear. This is your Friend and mine.

Cheer up! We are now nearer glory than when we first believed. There sits Jesus, once crowned with thorns, bruised and crucified for your sins and mine, in all His ineffable beauty and glory waiting to bid us welcome home. "Come, you who are blessed by my Father; take your inheritance, the kingdom prepared for you since the creation of the world." Heaven is not so far off as we think. It invites us; and it is but a step and we are there! This poor world is not our rest! Heaven is our home, and we are but sojourners here in this wilderness for a while, soon to be away! Cheer up!

Holy counsels to a young clergyman- The Holy Spirit must be your teacher. He alone can accompany His own Word spoken to the soul. He it is who gives life. He it is that convinces of sin, strips the sinner of his filthy rags, and applies the blood of Christ to the guilty conscience and speaks peace. Do not give the promises to the goats, which are intended only for the sheep! Here, my friend, make a distinction, lest any take the children's bread and are self deceived. I have seen a whole congregation addressed as believers, while fully two thirds or more were unconverted! Oh, how awful is such a deception! Oh, preach with your eye upon eternity! Preach the gospel as though Jesus were at your side! Think of the never dying souls around you, unawakened, insensible, led captive by Satan at his will. Work for Christ. Be much in prayer. Go to Jesus for all your supplies. "Without me you can do nothing." Get your message from Him. Great is your work! Vast is your responsibility! You are in yourself powerless, but He is all power, and is ready to give you all you need. Carry your empty vessel to His overflowing fountain of living grace!

Pray in prayer. Oh, how many unmeaning, heartless prayers are offered up that never reach the ear or heart of God!

Praise and laud His holy name for all His mighty goodness and rich display of love to us, poor lost sinners! It was love that carried Him through His deep degradation and sorrow, and that transfixed Him to the cross! It was boundless, matchless love from first to last! Oh, should we not live for Him! I think if I had ten thousand hearts, I would give them all to Him! May the Lord bless you with much of His presence, and shed abroad His own precious love in your heart!

Dear friend, do you feel Jesus precious to your soul? Is He not the fountain, yes, the ocean of love? Oh, get much of His love into your heart! Aim to live on high! The soul naturally, through the weakness of the flesh, cleaves to the dust; and Satan is ever busy in encumbering our minds with the poor world we are rapidly passing through. Well may he be called the "god of this world." Do not be ignorant of his devices.

While passing through all the daily changes of life, we should call to mind that, either sooner or later, we are hastening to the great and most eventful change that will take place. The world, with Satan at its head, will be incessantly calling off our attention to the poor trifles of time, making every effort to occupy our thoughts, and so leave very few, if any, for the glory that awaits us above. Do we not daily see the extreme folly of taking up our rest here on earth?

On looking back upon the past of my eventful life, I can trace God's fatherly hand in all His correctings and disappointings, the crosses and losses by the way, and how needful they all were to bring me to seek all my good in Jesus; for in Him I find all my soul needs.

Oh, to have such a Friend to go to, who has all things at His command; the gold and the silver are His, and the cattle upon a thousand hills, and all hearts are His. Let there be no distance between you and Jesus. Live upon Him. Live for Him. Yes, live with Him even here. Cling to Him, for He is your life. Carry all your cares, little or great, to Him. He will listen to all. It is written, "Casting all your cares upon Him, for He cares for you." Do not let the poor trifles, the gewgaws of this trifling world entangle your heart's best affections. Look at this world as "passing away," and not worthy of a thought. Keep close to Jesus. He loves you. Oh, repay Him by giving Him your whole, your undivided heart! He will accept it just as it is, and make it all you may wish to have it.

Oh, this is a world full of snares, and our sinful hearts are so deceitful, they are ever ready to fall into them.

Dear child of God, Jesus' loving eye is ever upon you, and His loving heart is ever towards you.

Jesus is now, though in heaven, what He was when on earth. He is just as ready to bow down His loving ear, and listen to our faintest whisper, as He was when here in this world of sin and sorrow. He was never known to turn one away that came to Him for help. He is the same now; full of the tenderest sympathy; and He needs us to deal with Him as helpless children, who can do nothing of ourselves that is good, and need to be led and upheld every step we take in this sinful and treacherous world.

The purity of heaven is sweetly attractive, and, next to being with Jesus, will make heaven what it is, a place of perfect happiness. It is sin that creates all our sorrow here on earth.

Truly, all whose eyes the Lord has opened must say this is a world of sorrow. Trials, in endless forms- crosses, sickness, temptations; assail us at every step we take through this wilderness. But we look for better things to come. The Lord is too good to put us off, even with the best of this poor world. For what is the best of it? If we had health, riches, and all the honor of a princely throne, what would they avail us? We are appointed to die, and a better world, or a worse world, is prepared for us.

I am unworthy of the least crumb of mercy that falls from His own dear, loving hand.

Remember, all the way you are led is chalked out for you by infinite wisdom; and in that covenant that is ordered in all things and sure. Not a step we take but is ordered by infinite love. All our chastenings and rebukes are so many precious tokens of our adoption into the family of God. Unbelief would often suggest hard thoughts of Him whose heart is always love towards us; but He, seeing the best way for each to attain to that blessed preparation for the full enjoyment of what He has gone to prepare for us, deals with us as seems in His infinite wisdom to be the best. Then, let us hush every murmur, or desire to have our own way, seeing that the Lord's way must be the best way. When we get above, we shall then study all the way He has led us, and admire and adore the wisdom that condescended to take such care of us, and at last to make all our trials, crosses, and losses, to work together for our good and His glory.

May we never forget that God's glory is connected with every step a saint of God takes through the wilderness.

How sweet it is to look above and beyond this transient valley of tears! This is not our rest, because it is polluted. There is no sickness in heaven; no desponding feelings there; all love, enjoyment, and blessedness.

How is our loving, gracious God dealing with you? In all His dealings, whatever they may be, there is nothing but the tenderest love towards you, all designed to draw you nearer and nearer to Himself. We are tried in order to bring us to a better acquaintance with His tenderness, sympathy, and unchanging love. He cares for you. You need not trouble yourself about, or load yourself with, earthly cares. Carry them, as they arise, to Him. Do not fret yourself about managing matters, when He, who has sent the cares, will manage better for you than you can for yourself. Come with an open heart, and pour all into His own loving heart. This is the confidence He loves. What a mercy to have such a God and Father to deal with us, who pities and loves us too! Oh, let us rejoice together, and cast all our cares upon Him, and be anxious for nothing.

Do not be concerned with all the tinsel glory of this empty, unsatisfying world. It is not worth a straw when compared with what awaits us! What an unsatisfying world this is, to have our all in! How trifling does everything appear which is not in some way connected with God's glory. Look upon all you now see or admire as passing away, yourself passing away with it. This world is a waste land, a howling desert! Oh, that we did but consider it as such, and expect nothing in it but thorns and thistles; looking unceasingly, with the anticipation of holy joy, to the period when He shall say to us, "Come away, my love, my fair one, enter into the joy of your Lord!"

Go to Jesus when you will, you will be always welcome, and never more so than when you come full of needs. You may tire a fellow creature out with your often coming, but you will never weary Jesus, your own Jesus, that Brother born for your adversity. Recollect you can, at all times, and under all circumstances, in the streets, in company, abroad, or at home, have the loving, listening ear of Jesus! What an honor is this put upon a poor worm! Whatever concerns you, equally concerns Christ.

What poor creatures we are if left to ourselves! What a mercy there is One that loves us better than we love ourselves, and will watch over us all our journey here, and who has engaged (by all the varying dispensations of His providence) to prepare us for that blessed place He has gone to prepare for us. And oh, what a place will that be! Love Him supremely! Live for eternity! Live for Jesus! Have much to do with Him!

Live for eternity! This world is not worth living for. Its honors, its riches, its glories are things ever passing away; but the love of Jesus is eternal as Himself. Oh, live for eternity! The glory of this world is fading, and is soon gone, and gone forever! Again I say, live for a glorious eternity! If you could have the glory, the wealth, and the honors of this world laid at your feet, short would be the empty enjoyment of them. Then, live and act with reference to eternity! And oh, the glory that awaits the true follower of Christ, who has cast overboard all that the world calls good and grand, and taking the Bible as his directory, walks as Jesus did.

Let us keep very near to Jesus. Be much in close communion with Him. While we tell Him all that is in our hearts, He will unfold His own tender loving heart to us. How He loves us! It is His glory and delight to do us good. We must die before we can know how much He loves. He is watching over us moment by moment; and there is not a pain or a trial but by its discipline He is preparing us for that dwelling above, which His infinite love has prepared for us, and which He will have us in the full enjoyment of.

We need not fear the prospect of changing worlds-earth for heaven; sin for holiness; and the disappointing creature for the overflowing fountain of all goodness and love. That world we hope to go to is worthy of all our thoughts and best affections.

I can truly say I love the Lord. But oh, how little in proportion to His love to me!

Who could or would have borne with us as Jesus has done? He has led and kept us, loving us in spite of all that was so unlovely in us.

What a change from a bed of suffering at once into the presence of Christ! Oh, let us make and sustain a close acquaintance with Christ here, that we may not feel we are going to a stranger when we depart, but to be with one with whom we have had close communion and heavenly communion here below.

Truly we live in a dying world! We see one another pass away out of sight, and yet how little impression it makes upon the survivors!

What a mercy to know that all these events which seem confusion to us are, even now, accomplishing His own eternal plans and purposes of love. Oh to trust Him fully, and watch His providence in all that is transpiring.

Is it not a blessed thing to know that God has to do with us, and that we have to do with God, every moment of our fleeting existence? How precious is the thought! I would not desire it otherwise for millions of worlds! It is the joy of my heart by night and by day. How sweetly and securely can I travel through all the intricate mazes of this wilderness state, while I feel that God is with me, that His eye is upon me, and His heart toward me.

Oh, to be more alive to eternal things, and to sit loose to the things that are passing away daily. We too much magnify present trifles, and dwell too little upon the glory that awaits us above. And yet, in one moment, we may be put into possession of our glorious inheritance. What a heaven awaits us! What glory is before us! Jesus standing ready to receive us! Let us encourage each other in the way. We shall soon be at home; our happy home; no home like it here. It is sweet in prospect! Absent from the body, present with the Lord!

Blessed be God for all the rich supplies afforded us in this wilderness.

Such a Friend is Christ to us- always ready to help us, to strengthen us, to comfort us when we are cast down, and to lift us above the base cares of time, and to speak sweet peace to our too often failing and doubting hearts. Unbelief, cruel unbelief, destroys more than half our comforts while on our short passage to glory.

A little while and we shall be put into possession of our glorious inheritance; and all our poor, short lived trials, crosses, and disappointments are so many rich blessings in disguise to prepare us for it. What a hope we have of being shortly with Jesus! Oh that we might be kept disentangled from the rubbish of this fallen world! In a fallen house we must expect a great deal of rubbish; such are the poor trifles of this contaminating world by which we are so often engrossed, and through which we are so rapidly passing.

Oh, to look forward more! Are we not too much like children playing with toys, and when they are broken, sitting down and mourning over them? Let us keep our hearts near to Jesus, so as to be quite willing to depart and be with Him.

We trifle too much with our God!

God will not put us off with the worldling's trash. He has higher enjoyments for His children.

What a poor, unsatisfying world is this! While we have cause to be grateful; oh, how grateful; for the accommodation afforded us while here, yet what a mercy of mercies we are not to live here always! Oh, the goodness of God, to prepare us for, and point us to, a better world! My soul is often overwhelmed at the thought of it, and how very soon I shall be there in its full enjoyment.

Dear friend, think more of that eternity to which day by day we are hastening, and less of this world we are so soon to leave.

Jesus is watching over us with an ever watchful eye. Oh, to know that He loves us, that His love never changes, that He is causing all things to work together for our best interests, and in due time will come and receive us unto Himself, and that when we see Him we shall be like Him! What a thought is that for a poor sinner; to be like the Son of God; the Son of the Highest; the Great Jehovah! Oh, if I had a thousand hearts I would give them all to Jesus!

What a mercy that Jesus is ever with us, by day, by night, in sickness, in health, in time, and through eternity! "I will never leave you nor forsake you." But we live in a changing world. The creature changes, we change, but, "I the Lord, do not change." Ever the same loving, faithful friend is Jesus. Bless the Lord for this, O my soul! I live in Him, and I desire to live for Him, and with Him, even here, as far as I can, in the body. But oh, the joy of knowing and feeling, that before long I shall be with and like Him forever! How great the bliss, even in anticipation, of beholding Him face to face!

Often my aged heart seems to spring into youth again at the prospect of being with Jesus; seeing Him face to face; sitting at His feet; beholding Him as He is. I am favored sometimes with glimpses of the coming glory, a look into heaven now and then, a little anticipative realization of the presence of Him who will make heaven what it will be to us.

Dear friends, live above a dying world and all its fading things. It is not worth a thought. Live independently of the creature, and walk hand in hand with Jesus. Keep an open heart with Him, confiding to His love all you feel or fear. He will not betray your confidence, but will lead you safely along the right road to glory; glory begun here, and increasing through the countless ages of eternity.

Made in the USA
San Bernardino, CA
15 August 2018